Pidgins and Creoles

W9-BTJ-807

Language and Society

General editor

John Spencer
Director,
Institute of Modern English Language Studies,
University of Leeds

Pidgins and Creoles

Loreto Todd

School of English, University of Leeds

Routledge & Kegan Paul
London and Boston

Wingate College Library

First published in 1974
by Routledge & Kegan Paul Ltd
Broadway House, 68–74 Carter Lane,
London EC4V 5EL and
9 Park Street
Boston, Mass. 02108, U.S.A.

Set in 10 on 11 point Times Roman
and printed in Great Britain by
Butler & Tanner Ltd, Frome and London

© Loreto Todd 1974

No part of this book may be reproduced in
any form without permission from the
publisher, except for the quotation of brief
passages in criticism
ISBN 0 7100 7865 X (c)
ISBN 0 7100 7927 3 (p)

084664

General Editor's preface

It is entirely appropriate that this first volume in the *Language and Society* series should be devoted to pidgins and creoles. In the broad interdisciplinary spectrum covered by sociolinguistics, no sector has developed so rapidly or proved more fruitful of debate and controversy. For long disregarded by most linguistic scholars as marginal to their interests, derided by speakers of the European languages which contributed to their origins, pidgins and creoles now turn out to pose many central and teasing problems for the student of language and society.

Their study has a natural and particular relevance for the communities which use them, and their continuing role in changing societies raises practical and often delicate questions of a social and educational nature. Those for whom they are mother tongues, or who utilize them as a convenient lingua franca, have been, for the most part, victims in the long process of domination and exploitation which has marked much of Europe's contact with the rest of the world during the past five centuries. In this sense these languages are part of the linguistic and cultural history of European expansion overseas.

But they also raise issues of a more searching and general kind. Linguistic history, as traditionally presented by philologists, normally focuses attention on standard forms exemplified in written texts; and the resulting impression is of a smooth organic development, to be understood and documented with scant reference to any interplay of social forces. Pidgins and creoles, on the other hand, emerge in conditions of social and ethnic turbulence, in situations of sharp cultural and linguistic confrontation, and without benefit of literacy. They are communicative tools forged and shaped under stress, whether in slave plantation, trading post, polyglot city or army camp. The very nature of their structure and lexical resources compels attention to the social and cultural circumstances of their origin, transmission and persistence. The question must arise as to whether we may have overlooked similar conditions and consequences at certain stages in the history of many of the languages of the world.

The study of these linguistic poor relations of the great language families, bred in harsh and limiting conditions, may yet have much to tell us about the nature of human interaction through language, and about man's innate communicative competence. The radical restructuring of linguistic elements so evident in the formation of pidgins and creoles may offer some clues as to the inherent and universal properties of all human language. Here, as elsewhere in this developing field of study, debate and disagreement abound.

The author of this volume, Loreto Todd, is eminently qualified for her task. A leading British specialist in creole studies, she has much research experience and extensive knowledge of the specialized literature. Several years in Cameroon gave her the opportunity to investigate at first hand the local variety of West African Pidgin, and to gain a fluent mastery of it. Since her appointment to the University of Leeds some years ago she has extended this experience by visits to Africa, the Caribbean area and Papua New Guinea, and through contacts with research workers elsewhere. In presenting the various aspects of her subject she has been able to draw richly on her own wide comparative knowledge of pidgin and creole languages in various parts of the world, as well as on a large body of published and unpublished material by other scholars.

Sociolinguistics is a large and expanding field of interdisciplinary activity, focusing attention in a variety of ways on the interaction of linguistic and social phenomena. For students in a broad range of humane disciplines it can offer new and stimulating perspectives. It is the purpose of this series to offer brief, readable and scholarly introductions to the main themes and topics covered by current sociolinguistic studies.

John Spencer

Contents

Preface   xi

Chapter one   Introduction   1

      two   Language and name   12

    three   Theories of origin: pidgins   28

     four   The process of development: from
            pidgin to creole   50

     five   The scope of pidgins and creoles   70

      six   Conclusion   87

Appendix one List of pidgins and creoles referred to
              and area of use   93

        two   List of less well-known languages referred
              to and area of use   95

      three   Source of proverbs quoted   96

            Suggestions for further reading   98

            Bibliography   100

Illustrations

Maps

1   The widespread nature of the pidgin/creole
    phenomenon   8
2   (a) Atlantic pidgin and creole Englishes   14
    (b) Pacific pidgin and creole Englishes   14

Preface

In writing about pidgins and creoles one could take as one's subject matter the whole history of societies and cultures in contact, but to do so would mean producing a book of unmanageable proportions or a survey so cursory and so superficial as to be of limited value. Instead of speculating, therefore, about the distant past, instead of attempting to probe and penetrate the hundreds of pidgins and creoles that exist today, I shall limit the scope of this book to a consideration of those which seem to have arisen since the fifteenth century, when first Portugal and then the other European nations began to sponsor voyages of discovery; in particular, attention will be focused on those pidgins and creoles which are 'English-based', that is, lexically related to English. This delimitation allows one to analyse the subject in some depth, though the magnitude of even this task becomes clear when one realizes that mutually unintelligible varieties of pidgin English exist in Hong Kong and Honduras, Nigeria and Papua New Guinea.

One of the biggest problems facing anyone writing about pidgins and creoles is the choice of orthography, because standard orthographies exist for very few of these languages. In the interests of simplicity I have avoided an over-use of phonetic symbols. Forms will be cited in the orthography of the work they occur in, but the following conventions will be adhered to in all discussion of and reference to unwritten sources, or sources which lack a consistent orthography:

i — has the value of the vowel sound in 'meat'

e — has a value closer to French 'é' as in 'thé' than to any English vowel, though it is less tense than 'é'

ε — has approximately the same value as the vowel sound in 'get'

a — represents a sound similar to the 'a' in French 'pas'

$ɔ$ — is similar to the vowel sound in 'not'

o — resembles the Scottish pronunciation of the vowel sound in 'go'

u — has approximately the same value as the vowel sound in 'rule'

ei — is similar to the vowel sound in 'day'

ai — has the value of the vowel sounds in 'I', 'high'

au — is similar to the vowel sound in 'house'

$ɔi$ — has the sound of 'oy' as in 'toy'

Where vowels are doubled in the text it means that the vowel in question has extra length; e.g. the vowel sound in the first syllable of *naada* differs in length only from the vowel sounds in *nada*. In the interests of consistency consonants are always given the same notation in references to pidgins and creoles. In most instances the consonantal sounds in the various pidgins and creoles are similar to their English equivalents but the following orthographic conventions will be adhered to:

ch — always has the value of the 'ch' in 'chin' and never of the 'ch' in 'machine'

sh — always has the value of 'sh' as in 'sheep'

j — always has the value of the 'j' in 'just'

y — always has the value of the 'y' in 'you'

ny — is similar to the opening sound of the English pronunciation of 'new'.

Chapter one

Introduction

trɔki wan fait bɔt i sabi sei i han shɔt!   (Tortoise wants to fight but he knows his arms are short), i.e. Know your limitations!

Pidgins and creoles are today to be found in every continent. References to their existence go back to the Middle Ages and it is likely that they have always arisen when people speaking mutually unintelligible languages have come into contact. Yet what are they? It is convenient to begin with the useful myth that one can give short, neat definitions of the terms 'pidgin' and 'creole', though it is worth stressing from the outset that the many-faceted nature of human languages is unlikely to be encapsulated in a few sentences. In a very real sense, the entire book is the definition, and the full nature of pidgins and creoles will emerge only gradually.

Pidgins and creoles have been given both popular and scholarly attention. Popularly, they are thought to be inferior, haphazard, broken, bastardized versions of older, longer established languages. In academic circles, especially in recent years, attempts have been made to remove the stigma so frequently attached to them by pointing out that there is no such thing as a primitive or inferior language. Some languages, it is true, may be more fully adapted to a technologically advanced society but all languages are capable of being modified to suit changing conditions. Yet, while scholars have increasingly come to recognize the importance of pidgin and creole languages, there has been considerable debate, and disagreement, among them as to the precise meaning to be attached to the terms. The following definitions would, however, be widely accepted as a reasonable compromise.

A *pidgin* is a marginal language which arises to fulfil certain restricted communication needs among people who have no common language. In the initial stages of contact the communication is often limited to transactions where a detailed exchange of ideas is not required and where a small vocabulary, drawn almost exclusively from one language, suffices. The syntactic structure of the pidgin is less complex and less flexible than the structures of the languages which were in contact, and though many pidgin features clearly reflect usages in the contact languages others are unique to the pidgin. A comparison of contemporary pidgin Englishes, such as, for example, those in Papua New Guinea (PNG) or in Cameroon, with English shows that the pidgins have discarded many of the

Table 1

French	English	Neo-Melanesian	Cameroon pidgin
je vais	I go	*mi*	*a*
tu vas	you go	*yu*	*yu*
il/elle va	he/she/it goes	*em*	*i*
nous allons	we go	*yumi* *mipela* } *go*	*wi* } *go*
vous allez		*yupela*	*wuna*
ils/elles vont	they go	*ol*	*dem*

inessential features of the standard variety, as two brief illustrations should clarify. All natural languages have some degree of redundancy. In many European languages, for example, plurality is marked in the article, the adjective and the noun, as well as, occasionally, by a numeral. In 'l*es deux* grand*s* journ*aux*' there are, in the written form, four overt markers of plurality, three in the spoken form. English is, in this respect, less redundant than French, but in the comparable phrase 'the *two* big newspaper*s*' plurality is marked by both the numeral and the noun ending. Neo-Melanesian (the pidgin English of PNG) and Cameroon pidgin are less redundant still, marking plurality by the numeral only, *tupela bikpela pepa* and *di tu big pepa*. The second example of discarding grammatical inessentials is illustrated in Table 1. English has less verbal inflection than French but both pidgins have an invariable verb form.

A *creole* arises when a pidgin becomes the mother tongue of a speech community. The simple structure that characterized the pidgin is carried over into the creole but since a creole, as a mother tongue, must be capable of expressing the whole range of human experience, the lexicon is expanded and frequently a more elaborate syntactic system evolves.

A creole can develop from a pidgin in two ways. Speakers of a pidgin may be put in a position where they can no longer communicate by using their mother tongues. This happened on a large scale in the Caribbean during the course of the slave trade. Slaves from the same areas were deliberately separated to reduce the risk of plotting and so, often, the only language common to them was the variety of the European tongue they had acquired on the African coast, or on board ship or while working on plantations. Children born into this situation necessarily acquired the pidgin as a first language and thus a creole came into being. But a creole is not always the result of people being deprived of the opportunity to utilize their mother tongue. A pidgin can become so useful as a community lingua franca that it may be expanded and used even by people who share a mother tongue. Parents, for example, may use a pidgin so extensively throughout the day, in the market, at church, in offices and on public transport, that it becomes normal for them to use it also in the home. In this way children can acquire it as one of their first languages. This second type of creolization can probably occur only in multilingual areas where an auxiliary language is essential to progress. There is evidence that such creolization is taking place in and around Port Moresby and in other mixed communities in PNG, where Neo-Melanesian has for many a prestige status. Wolfers points out that 'many New Guineans regard the learning of the pidgin as the most important turning point in their lives, when, for the first time, they are able to look for work outside their home areas. A knowledge of the language is still one sure way of gaining prestige as an educated man, and one capable of dealing with Europeans in some areas of the territory' (1971, p. 415). A similar phenomenon is observable in Cameroon where, in the multilingual south-western area, pidgin has been the most useful lingua franca from at least as far back as 1884 when the German administration of the country began. So entrenched was pidgin English even then that the Germans had to issue a pidgin English phrase book to facilitate communication between their soldiers and the Cameroonians. In this area, as Rudin indicates, 'there were so many dialects that the various tribes spoke and still do speak Pidgin English, to make themselves understood in their periodic market days' (1938, p. 358). Today, pidgin English is even more widespread in the area and its very usefulness often makes it the language of choice even among speakers of the same mother tongue, and some children now use it as a first language.

In theory, the distinction between a pidgin and a creole is clear: a pidgin is no-one's first language whereas a creole is. But this distinction is sociological rather than linguistic, as reference to specific cases shows. The so-called Cameroon pidgin, even where it is not a mother tongue, is not restricted to any region, class, occupation or semantic field. It is the vehicle for songs, witticisms, oral literature, liturgical writings and sermons, as well as being the most frequently heard language in the area. In all these functions it parallels Krio, the English creole of Sierra Leone, which is the mother tongue of about two hundred thousand speakers in and around Freetown. Since both languages are equally capable of serving all the linguistic requirements of their speakers it is hard to draw a linguistic line between them, though it can be pointed out that many Krio speakers use no other language whereas most speakers of Cameroon pidgin speak at least one Cameroonian vernacular as well.

An interesting point about European-language-based creoles, that is creoles which have European tongues as their lexical source language, is that their history is known. There is sufficient historical documentation to make it clear that they have developed from a contact pidgin which was subsequently adopted as a mother tongue. But if their history had not been known it is a matter of considerable debate whether they could, on linguistic evidence alone, be distinguished from other mother tongues. Such a consideration allows one to speculate that pidginization and creolization may have been much more prevalent in language change than linguists have hitherto acknowledged. It would be interesting to probe the changes Latin underwent in being transmuted into French. Did a pidgin Latin develop to facilitate communication between the Romans and the Gauls? Was it subsequently extended and creolized? Or was there already in the Roman army a simplified, common denominator Latin, from which dialectally divergent elements had been strained? Did a creolized Latin develop as a result of intermarriage? And was it continually influenced by the prestige of Latin, growing closer to it while still preserving features of the original pidgin? Such considerations cannot be fully explored in this book; but even posing the questions allows one to speculate that internationally respected languages like French may well have undergone similar processes to those which can be observed in the world's present pidgins and creoles.

In this study the distinction between a pidgin and a creole will continue to be made according to whether or not the language is the mother tongue of a speech community, but in this case, a further subdivision of pidgins is required. Pidgins are auxiliary languages which can be characterized as either 'restricted' or 'extended'. A restricted pidgin is one which arises as a result of marginal contact such as for minimal trading, which serves only this limited purpose and which tends to die out as soon as the contact which gave rise to it is withdrawn. A good example of this type of pidgin is what has been called Korean Bamboo English. This was a very restricted form of English which gained a limited currency between Koreans and Americans during the Korean war. It has by now almost disappeared, though a similar variety is reported to have developed in Vietnam. An extended pidgin is one which, although it may not become a mother tongue, proves vitally important in a multilingual area, and which, because of its usefulness, is extended and used beyond the original limited function which caused it to come into being. There is reason to believe that the many West African pidgins and creoles attained their present extended range of use because, having come into being as a

P C—B

result of contact between white and black, they were soon used and further developed in multilingual areas between black and black.

People in the western world tend to think in terms of standard, written languages and spoken forms closely related to these and strongly influenced by them. But in many parts of the world, even today, literacy is often rare and language standardization unknown. Such conditions were more common in the past, and in many regions travellers had to grope their way, linguistically speaking, and quickly establish some means of communicating. The communication exchanges often resulted in the simplifying of the language(s) concerned. When the contact was between closely related languages processes of simplification and accommodation were at work but a wholesale discarding of inflection was neither necessary nor helpful. An example may clarify this point. When the Vikings and Anglo-Saxons came into linguistic contact they shared a similar grammar and a considerable lexical stock. Communication common denominators were close at hand and many features common to Germanic languages could be maintained. Yet Anglo-Saxon did undergo a process of simplification as a result of this contact, a process which differed in degree rather than essence from the process of extreme simplification which English has undergone in certain contact situations where pidgins have arisen.

Far from being mere jargons or bastardized versions of standard languages, today's pidgins and creoles may be attestations of what happens when, in societies not enslaved by the notion of literate standards, languages come into contact. They have resulted from the fusion of almost every possible combination of languages and occur in all inhabited areas of the world. In Europe Russenorsk, a pidgin now almost extinct, arose from the contact of two Indo-European languages, Russian and Norwegian, as a means of facilitating communication between Russian and Norwegian fishermen. In South America one finds many creoles, among them Surinam's Sranan, a creole which resulted from the contact of English and a variety of West African languages. In the Pacific, in

PNG, Police Motu arose from the contact between speakers of Motu and other Papuan vernaculars. It has recently expanded its vocabulary by adopting words from Neo-Melanesian. Chinook Jargon is now almost entirely restricted to Canada but in the nineteenth century it was spoken from Oregon to Alaska. This pidgin is thought to have developed from the contact of French and English with Chinook and Nootka; but there is still controversy over its origin (see Hancock, 1972, p. 3). In Africa, in the Central African Republic, the pidgin Sango developed due to the contact of Ngbandi with other African languages. Along the coast of China, in Shanghai and to a lesser extent in Hong Kong, one finds relics of the once widespread China Coast Pidgin English which arose as a result of the contact between English and coastal Chinese. These six cases are only a sample of the variety of possible combinations but they give some indication of how widespread the pidgin/ creole phenomenon is (see Map 1).

A final clarification may be useful in order to indicate the distinction between a pidgin variety of a language and a dialect. The pidgin/dialect dichotomy is one which requires attention because there are areas like Jamaica and Hawaii where the distinction is not easily drawn. It is true that in many cases dialectal differences can be explained without reference to historical contact with another language. In addition, the majority of dialects of English are mutually intelligible. Pidgin and creole varieties of English can, on the other hand, only be explained by reference to other languages and they are often mutually unintelligible, with each other and with standard international English. Again, an example can highlight these differences. Where standard English has 'I was standing at the corner gossiping', some dialect speakers in Leeds say 'I were stood at t' corner gossiping', and a Cameroon pidgin speaker would say *a bin tanap fɔ kɔna an a bin di kɔnggɔsa*. One can see that those who produce the first two sentences are using the same lexical and syntactic material in that they are both using a form of the sentence *I + past tense of BE + marked form of the verb STAND + prepositional noun phrase + gossiping*, whereas they differ from the pidgin sentence in both vocabulary and

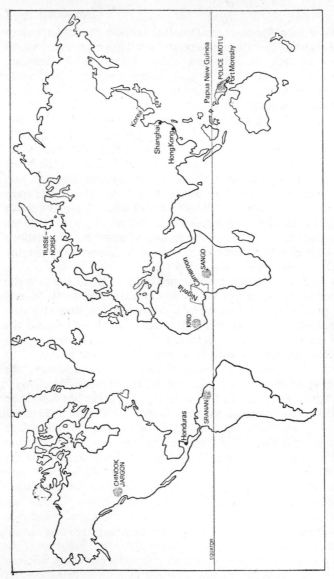

MAP 1 The widespread nature of the pidgin/creole phenomenon

syntax. One can only explain the occurrence of *kɔnggɔsa* by referring to the West African languages, including Twi, in which it means *gossip*.

Further examination of pidgins/creoles and dialects, however, indicates that the distinction is not always as clear as the above examples suggest. In Jamaica where the creole has been exposed to the regular and increasing influence of the standard international variety of English one can find a whole spectrum of Englishes, referred to as the 'post-creole continuum' and ranging from deep creole through creole-influenced forms to a regional variety of the international standard. As well as the standard *I didn't get the ball*, one can attest the following variations *mi no get di ball, mi neva get di ball, mi din get di ball, a neva get di ball, a din get di ball*. And, in Ireland, where the non-standard varieties of English are described as 'dialects' a similar spectrum exists, a spectrum showing different degrees of influence from Gaelic. Limiting oneself to syntactic difference one can range from the strongly influenced *Would you see does he be at himself in the evenings?* through a form, recognizable if still non-standard, *Would you see is he in good form in the evenings?* to the standard *Could you check to see that he is normally well in the evenings?*

While acknowledging the inherent similarities in certain pidgin/creole and dialect situations it may be remarked that the differences between Anglo-Irish and standard English can all be explained by reference to one language, Gaelic, but the differences between any extended pidgin or creole and standard English are much less easily identified. And, leaving aside for the moment language-influenced dialects of English, it can be said that all dialects of English, whether regional or social, share a large number of phonological, lexical and syntactic features with the standard form and that there is no area where two abutting dialects are mutually unintelligible. In PNG, however, a pidgin English does exist side by side with a standard Australian English, and that the two are mutually unintelligible is clear from the following soap powder advertisement in Neo-Melanesian: '*Olgeta harim gut! Dispela sop pauda, ol i kolim "Cold Power" i nambawan tru. Em i wasim na rausim tru ol kainkain pipia long ol klos bilong yu.*' ('Everybody listen closely! This soap powder, called "Cold Power" is definitely the best. It washes and completely removes all kinds of stains from your clothes') (*Wantok, pes 5, Trinde, Ogas 18, 1971—One-Language/Compatriot*, page 5, Wednesday, August 18, 1971).

It will become increasingly clear that pidgins and creoles are not simply dialects of English whose differences from the international standard can be explained in terms of regional and temporal distance. Pidgin and creole Englishes have arisen in multilingual situations where English has come into contact with structurally very different languages, where English has been so influenced by the other languages that the grammar of the pidgin which emerges is not just a simplified grammar of English or a simplified version of the grammar of the other languages. It is not even a common denominator grammar of the contact languages. Rather, the grammars of creoles and extended pidgins are a restructuring of the grammars that interacted. A grapefruit has much in common with both oranges and lemons but its taste is uniquely its own. In the evolution of pidgins, and thus of creoles, new languages have come into being. This fact allows one to suggest an interesting distinction between a pidgin English and a variety like Anglo-Irish. In creoles and extended pidgins one finds not a reduced, or partial, or corrupt form of the grammar of English but a new system, related to the contact languages but possessing unique features. In the case of Anglo-Irish, English has certainly been influenced by Gaelic but there has been no drastic restructuring of its grammar, partly because the contact was between two languages only and partly because the pressure from standard British English has been uninterrupted and all-pervasive. One can therefore specify three main varieties of English apart from the international norm: 'dialects' where regional and/or social differences occur, 'dialects' where English has been influenced by another language, and pidgin and creole Englishes where the grammars of English and other languages have come into contact and been restructured in a new though related language.

In an introduction one has, of necessity, to skim the surface of the subject. In consequence, emphasis on certain points may temporarily force others out of focus. It has been suggested that the process of pidginization, that is the manoeuvres towards simplification which take place whenever and wherever people of linguistically different backgrounds are brought suddenly into contact, is not an unusual or exotic occurrence. The process, though usually short-lived, may be observed in markets frequented by foreigners, at tourist hotels, on guided tours; wherever, in fact, people who have elementary communication needs but possess only a vestigial grasp of each others' languages, come into contact. But the creation of a pidgin and its elaboration into either an extended pidgin or a creole, while not uncommon, is much rarer than the actual process of pidginization itself. The emergence of such a language as a permanent form is not merely the result of languages coming into contact and influencing each other; rather it is the birth of a new language, one with the potential to develop and spread or to disappear if the need for the communication which brought it into existence should cease to be operative.

Chapter two

Language and name

bɔn mi, a fiba yu (Born me, I favour you), i.e. If you give birth to me, I'll resemble you.

When one attempts a linguistic classification of pidgins and creoles one faces a very real problem. Considered from the point of view of their vocabularies all pidgin and creole Englishes are closely related to each other and, through English, to the Indo-European family of languages (see Table 2).

Table 2

English	Krio	Cameroon pidgin	Jamaican creole	Sranan	Neo-Mel
arm/hand	*an*	*han*	*han*	*ana*	*han*
back	*bak*	*bak*	*bak*	*baka*	*baksait*
blood	*blɔd*	*blɔd*	*blɔd*	*brudu*	*blut*
head	*ed*	*hed*	*hɛd*	*ede*	*het*
stomach	*bɛlɛ*	*beli*	*bɛli*	*bele*	*bel(i)*
ask	*aks*	*aks/as(k)*	*(h)aks*	*aksi*	*haskim*
come	*kam*	*kɔm*	*kɔm*	*kɔm*	*kam*
give	*gi*	*gi(f)*	*gi*	*gi*	*gifim*
go	*go*	*go*	*go*	*go*	*go*
take	*tek*	*tek*	*tek*	*teki*	*tekewei*

An examination of the syntactic evidence, however, suggests the need for caution in their classification. In certain structures, for example, French creoles and English pidgins and creoles of West Africa and the West Indies resemble each other more closely than they resemble the standard languages to which they are lexically related (see Tables 3 and 4). And such apparent conflict raises the interesting question of whether linguists should follow the syntactic evidence and co-classify languages whose lexicons would otherwise separate them, a

Table 3

English	Cameroon pidgin	French	Haitian creole
he/she is bigger than you	*i big pas yu*	il/elle est plus gros que vous	*li gro pas u*

Table 4

English	Krio	French	Seychellois
it's not very hard	*i no tu had*	ce n'est pas très difficile	*i pa tro difisil*

question which will receive further attention in chapter 3 in connection with theories relating to the genesis of pidgin and creole languages.

In the Introduction it was pointed out that there are many mutually unintelligible varieties of pidgin and creole Englishes in the world, as the versions of St Mark in Table 5 emphasize. Yet, in spite of the extensive differences that separate some pidgin and creole Englishes, one can still indicate similarities,

Table 5

English	Neo-Melanesian	Cameroon pidgin
And John was clothed with camel's hair,	*Na Jon i save putim klos ol i bin wokim long gras bilong kamel,*	*Fɔ dat taim John i kros bin bi biabia fɔ kamel,*
and with a girdle of skin about his loins; and he did eat locusts and honey.	*na em i pasim let long namel bilong en; na em i save kaikai grasop wantaim hani bilong bus.*	*weti nkanda wei i bin di taiam fɔ i wes; den i chɔp bin bi lukɔs weti hɔni.* (ch. 1, v. 6)

Wingate College Library

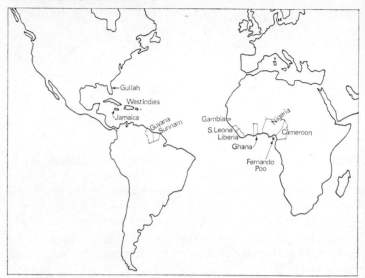

MAP 2   (a) Atlantic pidgin and creole Englishes

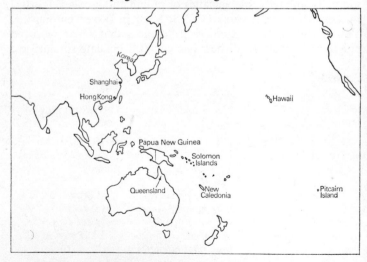

(b) Pacific pidgin and creole Englishes

over and above the lexical relationship. One can illustrate this most effectively by subdividing the pidgin Englishes of the world into two large classes, Atlantic and Pacific pidgins and creoles (see Map 2), because, while it is true that each of the languages has its individual traits, both subgroups have clear syntactic and historic connexions. All the Atlantic varieties, for example, have correspondences with West African coastal languages, correspondences which one would not expect to find in Pacific varieties. That the two subgroups are not entirely discrete, however, is suggested by the fact that the pidgin English in Hawaii has characteristics of both. It resembles the Atlantic varieties in its ability to use *bin* and *go* to indicate past and future time: *dɛm bin kɔm, dɛm go kɔm*—'they came, they will come', whereas its use of *-fela* as in *wanfela*—'one' links Hawaii unequivocally with the Pacific (see Todd, 1973).

Apart from the lexical similarities due to their core vocabularies deriving from English, all English pidgins and creoles make use of some Portuguese words. The Portuguese element varies from a few per cent in most cases to approximately 30 per cent in Saramaccan, a Surinam creole. All pidgin and creole Englishes, for example, possess a form of 'saber' for 'know' and of 'pequeno' for 'little' or 'offspring'.

When English-based pidgins and creoles are compared with English it becomes clear that there has been a reduction in the number of grammatical devices employed, and this is in spite of the fact that the pidgins occasionally develop distinctions which are not overtly marked in English. There are no synthetic plurals of the 'man/men' or the 'table/tables' type. Instead, in pidgins and creoles, nouns are invariable, like 'sheep'. In the Atlantic varieties plurality can be overtly marked by the postpositioning of *dem* immediately after the noun, thus *i get di buk dem*—'he has the books'. But plurality is normally implicit in the context (see Table 6). With pronouns there has been a reduction of the English system, oblique cases being frequently discarded (see Table 7).

It may be noticed, though, that both the Pacific and the Atlantic pidgins introduce distinctions which do not occur in standard English. Both have second person plural pronouns,

Table 6

English	Neo-Melanesian	Cameroon pidgin
one man/person	*wanpela man*	*wan man*
ten men/people	*tenpela man*	*ten man*
lots of men have no wives	*plenti man i no get meri*	*plenti man no get woman*

Table 7

Neo-Melanesian				Cameroon pidgin				
Person	Sing.	Pl.	Dual	Person	Sing.		Pl.	
					Nom.	Non-Nom.	Nom.	Non-Nom.
1	*mi*	*mipela*	*yumi*	1	*a/mi,a*	*mi*	*wi*	*wi*
2	*yu*	*yupela*		2	*yu*	*yu*	*wuna*	*wuna*
3	*em*	*ol*		3	*i*	*i/am*	*dem*	*dem/am*

Table 8

English	Neo-Melanesian	Cameroon pidgin
I came to the tree	*mi kam long diwai*	*mi, a bin kɔm fɔ stik*
have you a plate?	*yu get plet?*	*yu get plet?*
he/she/it is not carrying a bag	*em i no karim ruksak*	*i no di kari kwa*
we don't know how to shoot pigeons	*yumi* (you and I) *no sabi shut balus* *mipela* (me and others) *no sabi shut balus*	*wi no sabi shut pijɔn*
you (pl.) went to eat	*yupela go long kaikai*	*wuna bin go chɔp*
they went home	*ol i go long haus*	*dem bin go fɔ haus*

equivalent to non-standard 'yous', and Neo-Melanesian also makes a distinction, common in Austronesian languages, between 'we' meaning 'you and me' and 'we' meaning 'me and others not including you'. The sample sentences in Table 8 should make Table 7 more meaningful.

In pidgins and creoles gender distinctions are reduced or eliminated in both nouns and pronouns, though in some areas where English continues to be the official language a limited number of gender distinctions, especially the use of 'she/her', are being reintroduced. In nouns, natural gender can be marked by the use of *man/meri* in Neo-Melanesian, *man/woman* in Cameroon pidgin (see Table 9).

Table 9

English	Neo-Melanesian	Cameroon pidgin
hen	*paul meri* (<fowl+meii)	*woman fawu* (<woman+fowl)
cock	*paul man* (<fowl+man)	*man fawu* (<man+fowl)
girl	*pikinini meri*	*woman pikin*
boy	*pikinini man*	*man pikin*

There is no concordial agreement between subject and predicate in pidgins and creoles. Both noun and verb are invariable. Usually the form adapted from English is the base or unmarked form, the singular for nouns and the imperative for verbs. Occasionally, however, a marked form was adopted, as in *tit* for 'tooth/teeth' and *brok* for 'break', marked forms occurring in both Atlantic and Pacific varieties. Since the verb form is invariable, distinctions relating to time and continuity of action are either understood from the context or are indicated by adverbials or a set of free morphemes which precede the verb. In Neo-Melanesian and the Pacific varieties, with the exception of Hawaii, relationships of time and duration are rarely marked overtly, but where such distinctions are essential they are carried by means of adverbials like *baimbai* < 'by-and-by' for future reference, *pinish* < 'finish' for past:

baimbai i kam—'he'll soon come' and *i go, pinish*—'he has gone'. Besides distinctions which are contextually implied and besides the use of adverbials, most Atlantic pidgins and creoles have a set of free morphemes which can precede the unmarked verb indicating a range of subtle differences, a number of which are illustrated from Cameroon pidgin in Table 10.

Because pidgins and creoles are essentially non-written languages there is often a wide range of pronunciation, a range which reflects age, region and education in English. The number of distinctive vowel sounds used changes often from person to person and, although consonants are usually more stable, they too vary. In many West African pidgins 'l' and 'r' are free

Table 10

English	Cameroon pidgin
I am eating at the moment	*jɔsnau a di chɔp*
I have only just eaten	*a dɔng chɔp nau nau*
I ate yesterday	*yestadei a bin chɔp*
I'll eat tomorrow	*tumɔro a go chɔp*
I would have eaten if . . .	*a fɔ dɔng chɔp if . . .*

variables, and in the Pacific, the same is true of 'p' and 'f'. A compensation for the phonetic variability, however, is the greater syntactic regularity and the fixed word order. And, while it is true that the *alata/arata* < 'rat' type variation is still common in Cameroon and the *pis/fis* < 'fish' type common in Neo-Melanesian, international English is exerting a continuous pressure towards the acceptance of the form closest to the standard.

Most pidgins and creoles have a number of nautical words in their lexicons, reflecting the fact that the first contacts were often with sailors. Frequently, however, the nautical meaning has been modified. Krio's *gali* < 'galley' now refers to any kitchen, and throughout the pidgin/creole world *kago* < 'cargo' has taken on the meaning of any load, whether it is carried by hand, on the head or by some other form of transport. Forms of 'hammock' occur in both the Pacific and Atlantic areas and the same is true of 'capsize', usually with the more restricted meaning of 'spill', 'knock over'.

Serial verb structures occur more widely in pidginized languages than in their non-pidginized relations. The following example occurred in spontaneous dialogue in Cameroon pidgin: '*dat chif i woman i go stat bigin tich i, tɔk sei na so dem di mekam . . .*' ('that chief he woman he *go start begin teach* he, *talk say be* so they habitually make it; i.e. that chief's wife set out to teach her, saying this is how it is usually done . . .'). Such structures are considered useful indications of whether a language has been pidginized and their existence in Afrikaans (see p. 89) lends weight to the theory that Afrikaans is a creolized Dutch.

In the past, reduplication has been given undue prominence as a feature of pidgins and creoles. Most, if not all, languages utilize reduplication for emphasis. 'A big, big mountain' concentrates attention on the size, and is perfectly permissible in standard English. Pidgins and creoles in their use of reduplication differ from English in degree rather than in having introduced an entirely new method of intensifying meanings. When pidgin speakers had a limited vocabulary reduplication was a very simple method of extending it. In Pitcairnese, *ile* from 'hilly' has the same reference as in English whereas *ileile* refers to a 'choppy sea'; *drai* from 'dry' closely parallels English usage but *draidrai* is used to imply that food is 'unpalatable'. Reduplication, furthermore, served in all pidgins and creoles to distinguish between words whose pronunciations had coalesced. It was a valuable means of reducing an unacceptably high percentage of homophony. According to Krio's sound patterns 'sun' and 'sand' would both have become *san* and 'wash' and 'wasp' *was*. In Krio 'sun' remains *san* and 'sand' has become *sansan*, 'wash' continues to be *was* and a 'wasp' is *waswas*. And reduplication filled a third need. In early contacts pidgins made little use of synthetic comparatives like 'good/better/best'. Instead, reduplication was employed to express intensification, continuity, repetition. In Jamaican creole 'small' is *smal*, 'very small' is *smalsmal*. In Cameroon pidgin 'one' is *wan* while 'one by one' is *wanwan*, and in Neo-Melanesian 'talk' is *tɔk* but 'chatter' is *tɔktɔk*. It is clear that reduplication serves many purposes in English-based pidgins and creoles. Even where the vocabulary is small every word is potentially capable of being reduplicated. English can and does duplicate forms but not as extensively or as systematically as any of the pidgins and creoles. It would be hard, if not altogether impossible, to find in English a sentence comparable to one I recorded in Cameroon where an old man, lamenting the fact that his wife was perpetually scolding, exclaimed, *ene dei ene dei soso miamia* ('any day any day so so nagging').

Thus far in this chapter an attempt has been made to indicate the characteristics which pidgins and creoles share and which have resulted in their co-classification. But how did the terms 'pidgin' and 'creole' arise? How much can be discovered about their origins and use?

Although the term 'pidgin' is now widely accepted as a designation for simplified, auxiliary languages which have evolved to permit communication in multilingual areas, its etymology has never been satisfactorily explained. The most commonly held opinion is that given by the Oxford English Dictionary where a pidgin is defined as a 'Chinese corruption of English "business" used widely for any action, occupation or affair. Hence Pidgin-English, the jargon, consisting chiefly of English words, often corrupted in pronunciation, and arranged according to Chinese idiom, used for inter-communication between the Chinese and Europeans at seaports etc. in China, the Straits Settlement etc.' Even overlooking the fact that this definition is too narrow and prescriptive, it fails to account for the phonetic difficulties inherent in business/bizniz/ becoming/pidʒin/.

A second hypothesis was advanced by Leland in 1876 when he defined pidgin as 'business; affair; occupation; a word of very general application—e.g. *joss-pidgin*, religion; *chow-chow-pidgin*, eating or cookery. Probably the Chinese pronunciation of the word business... according to others of the Portuguese "ocupação" ' (p. 131). What makes the 'ocupação' suggestion so attractive is that the Portuguese were among the first European traders in West Africa, Asia and the Americas, and it is only reasonable to assume that some form of 'ocupação' was used with reference to 'trade, job, occupation'. That the Portuguese were not averse to using a simplified version of their language is evidenced by travellers to West Africa and Asia. In the early eighteenth century Barbot wrote of the 'broken Portuguese' of the Gold Coast (1746, p. 249) and in his book, published in 1727, Hamilton recorded: 'Along the sea coasts the Portuguese have left a Vestige of their language, tho' much corrupted, yet it is the Language that most Europeans learn first to qualify them for a general converse with one another, as well as with the different inhabitants of India' (Preface, p. xii). The form of 'ocupação' like the form of 'business' poses phonetic difficulties, difficulties relating to the loss of the first two syllables, to stress and vowel changes. Aphetism, or loss of initial syllables, is common in pidgins and creoles and examples of it occur in Leland's own Chinese pidgin English vocabulary where *lim* is listed as meaning 'eleven' (p. 127) and *pili* as 'emperor' (p. 131). But no acceptable explanation of the other phonetic changes has been advanced and so the 'ocupação' theory has received little support.

In 1959 Kleinecke (pp. 271–2) suggested an alternative etymology and place of origin for 'pidgin'. His hypothesis was welcomed because it involved only one very plausible sound change and because it helped to explain why 'pidgin' is international and not the sole preserve of the Chinese variety. Kleinecke claimed that 'pidgin' may derive from a Yayo (South American) form '-pidian', meaning 'people' and occurring in such tribal names as 'Mapidian', 'Tarapidian'. His claim is plausible on phonological, semantic and historical grounds. If 'pidgin' < 'pidian' can be traced back to the 1605–6 Oyapock settlement (near the Orinoco basin), its widespread use throughout the world might well be explained. Unfortunately, Kleinecke's theory rests on one solitary occurrence of 'Pidians'. Wilson wrote that when, in 1606, he joined Leigh, the

P C—C

commander of the expedition to South America, he found that the colonists were exhausted and even 'the Generall himselfe was very weak and much changed, which partly proceeded by reason of their great want of victuals, for that the Pidians could not at all times provide them that they wanted' (1625, p. 1260). A close examination of the 1625 text in which it occurs suggests that 'Pidians' might well be a misprint for 'Indians', a reference it clearly has in the context. In his account of the settlement Wilson uses 'Indian(s)' thirty-nine times, 'Pidians' once. The fact that other orthographic discrepancies appear, 'Arwakes', 'Arwalkes', 'Arwackes', lends weight to the suggestion that 'Indians' rather than 'Pidians' was intended. But, even allowing that the Oyapock colonists did refer to the variety of English used in dealing with the local people as 'pidian English', it is hard to explain why its usage then remains unrecorded for two hundred and twenty-five years until, in 1850, Berncastle uses 'pigeon' to designate the China coast variety of English (vol. 2, p. 65).

In 1972 a third source for 'pidgin' was suggested by Hancock. He pointed out that 'pequeno português' was a term used, at least in Angola, for the 'broken Portuguese spoken by illiterate Africans' (Moser, 1969). If, as seems likely in view of similar names for pidgins like 'petit nègre' and 'baby hollands', the term 'pequeno português' was once more widely used to refer to pidgin Portuguese, then 'pidgin' may well derive from a form of 'pequeno'—'little, offspring'. Such a view becomes phonetically more acceptable in view of Hancock's evidence that, in Sranan, a Surinamese creole, /pəçĩ/ and /ptʃĩ/ mean both 'little' and 'offspring'.

It is also possible that 'pidgin' derives from a Hebrew word 'pidjom' meaning 'barter'. The meaning is right, the sound change easy to account for, and Jewish immigration to the New World is attested from the seventeenth century, and in areas like Surinam, where the creoles are English-based. By the close of the seventeenth century three-quarters of Surinam's white population was made up of Jews (Rens, 1953 p. 22); and Edwards, writing of the British West Indies (1807, book 4, vol. 2, p. 3), could say:

I shall treat of each class separately; premising, however, that there are persons not comprehended in either class; such as emigrants from North America, and a considerable body of Jews. In Jamaica, the latter enjoy almost every privilege possessed by the Christian Whites, excepting only the right of voting at elections; of being returned to serve in the assembly, and of holding any office of magistracy; but they have liberty of purchasing and holding lands as freely as any other people.

That the term was employed by Jewish people is supported by Hassert's statement that 'Pidjom-Englisch nannte man das von den Bewohnern des Londoner Ghetto gesprochene Idiom' ('Pidjom-English was the name given to the idiom used by those who lived in the London ghetto') (1913, p. 432, fn. 2).

It is unlikely that one will ever learn exactly how and when the term 'pidgin' came to be applied to marginal languages. In any case, it is probably naïve to think in terms of one specific origin. 'Business', 'ocupação', 'pidian', 'pequeno' and 'pidjom' may all have contributed to the name now universally used. It is possible too that they were further reinforced by the English 'pigeon', especially if trade varieties of English were equated with parrot-like repetitions. That the spelling for the bird and the language were interchangeable is indicated by Leland's poem, 'The Pigeon' (1876, p. 74):

> One piecee pidgin makee nest
> Top-side one Joss-house up to sky, (i.e. church)
> One olo hen he wantchee know
> What for he pidgin lib so high?
> He pidgin talk, 'You savvy, flin, (i.e. friend)
> My eye make velly good look-see,
> Sometim to catchee chow-chow, or (i.e. food)
> When hawk come t'his side catchee me.'
> Suppose one man belongey smart,
> He allo-way catchee pidgin-eye;
> Who-man he makee good look-see,
> T'hat man he allo-way lisee high. (lisee—rise)

Forms of 'pidgin' may have arisen independently in the East and in the West which, because of their similarity of sound and reference, converged, thus reinforcing the term as a designate for a 'trade' or 'reduced' language.

If an incontrovertible pedigree cannot be provided for 'pidgin', is the situation any better with regard to 'creole'? The answer to this question is a qualified yes. The *OED* defines a creole as 'native to the locality, country; believed to be a colonial corruption of "criadillo", diminutive of "criado" bred, brought up, reared, domestic' and the 1972 Supplement adds the meaning of 'a creolized language'. There has, not unexpectedly, been considerable debate over the exact etymology of 'creole', but from the evidence it seems that the English form of the word comes from French 'créole', which is, in turn, derived from the Portuguese 'crioulo' rather than the Spanish 'criollo', though both Iberian forms are ultimately related to 'criar', which includes the meanings of 'to nurse, to breed, to nourish, to bring up.'

In 1590 de Acosta applied the term to those of Spanish blood born in the colonies, 'algunos criollos, como alla llaman los nacidos de las Espanoles en Indias' (some criollos, as they call those born of Spaniards in the Indies) (book 4, ch. 25, p. 278) and in 1609 de la Vega applied it to negroes to whom he incorrectly attributed the term (vol. 1, book 9, ch. 31, p. 607):

> The children of Spaniards by Spanish women born there (i.e.
> Peru) are called *criollos* or *criollas*, implying that they were born in the Indies. The name was invented by the Negroes, as its use shows. They use it to mean a Negro born in the Indies, and they devised it to distinguish those who come from this side and were born in Guinea from those born in the New World, since the former are held in greater honour and considered to be of higher rank because they were born in their own country, while their children were born in a strange land.

By 1697 Dampier could use the term to designate the English who were born in the colonies, referring to 'an English native of St Christophers, a Cirole, as we call all born of European parents in the West Indies' (book 1, ch. 4, p. 68). References in the eighteenth and nineteenth centuries seem to indicate a shift of emphasis from whites born in the colonies, to blacks born there, a shift emphasized by Bates's statement in 1863 that 'the term "creole" is confined to negroes born in the country' (p. 19). From the quotations cited one can see a referential development from someone/something native to an area, to a European born in the colonies, to all born there, to Africans born in the colonies; and, gradually, the meaning is extended to include the behaviour, social and linguistic, of creoles. It is not possible to say with absolute precision when the term 'creole' was first applied to the customs and language of those in the colonies; though the referential extension from the people to the language spoken by the people is an easy step, particularly if it was felt that the creoles spoke a modified version of an official standard. Mencken was utilizing the same type of extension when he preferred the term *The American Language* to the more widespread 'American English'. Lady Nugent, in her 1801–5 journal of her stay in Jamaica, talks of a creole breakfast: 'We breakfasted in the Creole style—Cassada cakes, chocolate, coffee, tea, fruits of all sorts, pigeon pies, hams, tongues, rounds of beef etc. I only wonder there was no turtle' (p. 55). If such breakfasts were typical it is not surprising that she referred to lounging around, unrestricted by work—or corsets—as 'creolizing' (p. 117). In addition, she refers to the 'Creole language' and from the context there is no suggestion of innovation in her diary entry, where she insisted that 'the Creole language is not confined to the negroes' (p. 98).

The term 'creole' is now mainly used in English to refer to languages which derive from pidgins and which, in many instances, share most of their vocabulary with a European language, usually English, French, Portuguese, Dutch and Spanish. Recently the meaning has been widened to include languages of similar type, though not related to European languages. Mbugu, for example, has been classified as a creole. It is a Tanzanian mother tongue, spoken by about 12,000 people but 'all that one can say with certainty about the origin of Mbugu is that at some time a Bantu and a non-Bantu language came into contact' (Goodman, 1971, p. 251).

Whether its reference was to people or languages the term 'creole' in the past frequently had pejorative overtones. Lady Nugent exemplifies this with regard to the Jamaican variety.

'The Creole language is not confined to the negroes. Many of the ladies who have not been educated in England, speak a sort of Broken English, with an indolent drawling out of their words, that is tiresome if not disgusting. I stood next to a lady one night, near a window, and, by way of saying something, remarked that the air was much cooler than usual; to which she answered, "Yes, ma'am, *him rail-ly too fra-ish*"' (p. 98).

Such condescending references to creoles, the languages and their speakers, can be quoted from every region of the world where a European-language-based creole or pidgin exists. As recently as 1953 Neo-Melanesian was referred to as 'inferiority made half articulate' and its grammar was attacked as being 'crude and incredibly tortuous' (see Hall, 1966, p. 106). To insist that such statements are unscientific, inaccurate, linguistically untenable, subjective and prejudiced does not alter the fact that, until very recently, pidgin and creole speakers have been made to feel ashamed of the language in which they could most easily express themselves. Theo Vincent, referring to Nigerian pidgin, claimed that 'at one time it was drummed into pupils at school that Pidgin was a debased form of English and so, many educated people who spoke it nevertheless tended to use it exclusively in familiar and private circles and only apologetically outside' (1972, p. 6). And this situation was by no means confined to Nigeria. Yet, in the past, when, out of shame, many speakers feigned ignorance of their creole mother tongues, there was often an ambivalent attitude to the creole. Describing the Haitian situation in 1959 Ferguson coined the term *diglossia* to describe the special form of bilingualism where two varieties of the one language exist in the same speech community, one of the languages having high status and the other low. In Haiti French was, and to a large extent still is, the language of prestige, education and culture; whereas the creole, the effective though not the official lingua franca, tends to be looked down on, and 'educated speakers of Haitian Creole frequently deny its existence, insisting that they always speak French' (p. 330). Yet certain Haitian proverbs underline the fact that it was the creole which was considered to be the language of honesty, truth and sincerity. Edith Efron has shown (1954, pp. 199–213) that *fai' la France* (to do as the French do) means 'to talk a lot and say nothing'; that *créole palé, créole comprenn* (creole spoken, creole understood) implies that 'true communication comes through creole'; and that *palé français* (speak French) carries the additional meaning of 'to offer a bribe'.

Although it would be inaccurate to suggest that the sense of shame and inferiority which creole speakers felt has disappeared entirely, evidence clearly shows that it is disappearing. Writing about the English-based creole of Antigua, Reisman can draw the conclusion that 'Creole is intrinsically felt to be the code of the genuine. School teachers, even head teachers, may, or may be forced to move into Creole to convince the children that they really mean what they are saying. Thus other forms of speech carry some aura of falseness' (1970, p. 140). And similar references could be quoted from many parts of the pidgin/creole world. Young, and especially educated, creole speakers are realising that there is no intrinsic stigma attached to speaking a creole, and that to deny their linguistic heritage is to interfere with their cultural heritage and to block, if not to dam, the flow of their self-expression.

This chapter has attempted to sketch in some of the linguistic characteristics which allow pidgin and creole languages to be co-classified. It has also tried to trace the origins of the terms 'pidgin' and 'creole' and show how they were modified and extended in meaning. But what caused them to come into being? Why were standard languages or existing dialects not acquired? Answers to these questions might well shed light on problems seemingly unconnected with pidgins and creoles. They might well provide information on how language is acquired and thus, indirectly, on 'the nature of human intelligence' (Chomsky, *Language and Mind*, 1968, p. 5), because, as Chomsky points out, the study of language and of its acquisition, is ultimately the study of the human mind.

Chapter three

Theories of origin: pidgins

yu tink sei na kapenta klin mi? (Do you think a carpenter cleaned/made me?), i.e. How do you think I came into being?

Although modern scholarship has amassed a considerable body of knowledge on the subject of pidgins and creoles, the further back one attempts to trace their history the more sketchy and speculative the account must be. In the past, they were seen as auxiliary languages, often regarded as debased jargons, so references to them are haphazard and random. Nevertheless, old manuscripts, especially sea journals and travellers' records, often indicate where and how these languages were used. Even more occasionally, samples of a pidgin or creole are cited, random samples like this reference from Bryan Edwards: 'A gentleman of Jamaica visiting a valuable Koromantyn-Negro that was sick, and perceiving that he was thoughtful and dejected, endeavoured to raise his drooping spirits. *Massa*, said the Negro (in a tone of self-reproach and conscious degeneracy) *since m'e come to White man's country me lub (love) life too much!* (1807, vol. 2, book 4, ch. 3, p. 83). One cannot build a theory on such evidence alone; but when supported by historical documentation and compared with samples of modern West Indian creoles, it can provide insights into the origins and development of such languages, insights which are of value in helping to explain the similarities which can be shown to exist between all the pidgins and creoles related to European languages.

In the Introduction and in chapter 2 it was suggested that, while pidginization may well be a natural consequence of languages in contact, the crystallizing of extended pidgins is much rarer. To date, scholars, in an attempt to explain both the genesis of and the similarities between these languages, have advanced four different and to some extent competing theories, an examination of which will provide the necessary background and perspective for a more economical and comprehensive hypothesis.

The baby-talk theory

Writing in 1876 about China coast pidgin English, Charles Leland explains certain features of the pidgin and concludes his Introduction with this remark: 'What remains can present no difficulty to anyone who can understand negro minstrelsy or baby talk.' He and many other travellers who heard pidgins and creoles were struck by the similarities these languages bore to the early efforts of children. They noticed that pidgin speakers and children often only approximated to the standard pronunciation, that they both used a high proportion of content words and relatively few function words, that in the speech of both morphological change was rare if not altogether absent, that word classes were much less rigidly established and that pronominal contrasts were frequently reduced. Many such similarities can still be shown to exist between child language and pidgins, and several scholars have called attention to this phenomenon in their attempt to explain how and why pidgins arose. Jespersen claimed (1922, p. 234) that similar results sprang from similar causes; in this case, the 'imperfect mastery of a language which in its initial stage, in the child with its first language and in the grown-up with a second language learnt by imperfect methods, leads to a superficial knowledge of the most indispensable words, with total disregard of grammar.'

Bloomfield also supported the baby-talk theory (1933, p. 472):

Speakers of a lower language may make so little progress in learning the dominant speech, that the masters, in communicating with them resort to 'baby-talk'. This 'baby-talk' is the masters' imitation of the subjects' incorrect speech. There is reason to believe that it is by no means an exact imitation, and that some of its features are based not upon the subjects' mistakes but upon grammatical relations that exist within the upper language itself. The subjects, in turn, deprived of the

correct model, can do no better now than to acquire the
simplified 'baby-talk' version of the upper language. The result
may be a conventionalized *jargon*. During the colonization of
the last few centuries, Europeans have repeatedly given jargonized
versions of their language to slaves and tributary peoples.

Nowadays, such an extreme viewpoint is rarely espoused
though occasional references to similar positions are still to be
found (see Wurm, 1971, p. 1000). It is quite likely that, in contact situations, some Europeans did attempt to simplify their
speech. But it seems to me highly dubious that they either
'deliberately and systematically simplified' it as Goodman
implied (1964, p. 124) or made a 'contemptuous imitation' of
the learners' 'jargon' (Bloomfield, 1933, p. 473). There is no
element of condescension in *Purchas his Pilgrimes* (1625)
where in chapter 3 of the fourth part, the Dominican Indians'
desire to learn English is related in this way (p. 1159):

> The last report of them shall bee what I have seene in experience,
> namely their great desire to understand the English tongue: for
> some of them will point to most parts of his body and having
> told the name of it in the language of Dominica, he would not
> rest till he were told the name of it in English, which having
> once told he would repeat till he could either name it right,
> or at least till he thought it was right, and so commonly it
> should be, saving that to all words ending in a consonant they
> always set the second vowel, as for *chinne*, they say *chin-ne*,
> so making most of the monasillables, dissillables.

This account does not suggest that the English deliberately
simplified their language though it does indicate that the
Dominicans, like most learners of a foreign language, tended
to interpret English according to the phonetic rules of their
own language.

As expounded in the past, the baby-talk theory reflected the
observations and the beliefs of many travellers and scholars,
but it has limitations. It fails to explain why pidgins are not
often mutually intelligible with the languages of which they
are, supposedly, baby-talk versions; more important, it fails to
explain why pidgins and creoles which are related to different
European languages are, in many ways, syntactically more

similar to each other than they are to the languages from which their lexicons derive. For example:

		Pronoun	Negator	Time marker	Unmarked verb form
Haitian créole	:	*li*	*pa*	*te*	*konẽ*
Cameroon pidgin:		*i*	*no*	*bin*	*sabi*

are closer to each other than to French 'il n'a pas connu/il ne connaissait pas' or English 'he didn't know'. Neither French-nor English-based pidgins or creoles have a copula in identifying sentences:

Haitian créole	:	*li bel*	—il/elle *est* beau/belle
Cameroon pidgin:		*i fain*	—he/she/it *is* handsome/fine

though both metropolitan varieties do. In addition, in both languages, interrogation is usually signalled by intonation alone whereas, in the related standards, there is normally a change in word order:

Haitian créole	:	*li bel?*	—est-il beau?/est-elle belle?
Cameroon pidgin:		*i fain?*	—is he/she/it handsome/fine?

The independent parallel development theory

Robert A. Hall, Jr was among the first scholars to recognize the pervading similarities apparent in the world's pidgins and creoles, yet he believes that many of them arose independently and developed along parallel lines. He and supporters of this theory believe that the similarities that exist can be accounted for by acknowledging that these languages all derive from Indo-European stock and, with regard to the Atlantic varieties, the majority of the speakers shared 'a common West African substratum' (1966, p. 77) and had to come to terms with similar physical and social conditions. While one cannot underestimate the validity of some aspects of this theory it has two main limitations. In the first place, structurally as well as lexically, the Atlantic and Pacific pidgin Englishes have common features which do not occur in standard English. They both, for example, use 'make' in giving polite orders. The equivalent of the English 'put out the fire' is *mekim dai faia* in

Neo-Melanesian and *mek yu lɔs faia* in Cameroon pidgin. Another similarity is their use of a form of 'too much' to mean 'very'. 'I'm very cold' becomes *mi kol tumas* in Neo-Melanesian and *mi, a kol tumɔs* in Cameroon pidgin. And the position of the sentence negator is identical in both languages, *mi no haskim* and *mi, a no bin ask* being the equivalents of 'I didn't ask'. Secondly, although it would be folly to deny the West African contribution to the Atlantic pidgins and creoles, one must not forget that the African slaves came from widely separated areas of West Africa and to overstress the similarity of their linguistic background is to oversimplify.

The nautical jargon theory

As early as 1938 John Reinecke suggested that a nautical jargon could have been the basis of many pidgins and creoles. This theory postulates that, until comparatively recently, ships had, of necessity, to develop a common denominator language because crews were generally composed of men speaking a variety of dialects and languages. There were, for example, fourteen different nationalities represented on Nelson's flagship *Victory*. According to supporters of this theory the sailors' lingua franca was passed on to Africans, Asians, Polynesians or whatever people the sailors came into contact with. The nautical jargon would thus have provided a nucleus for the pidgin, which would then have been expanded according to the model of the learners' mother tongue. Such an explanation helps to account for the similarities and dissimilarities that exist in the pidgin and creole Englishes of the world. The similarities are due to comparable nautical cores and the dissimilarities are due to the influences exerted by different mother tongues.

Evidence which supports this theory was collected by Matthews who points out that from the seventeenth century onwards sailors were renowned for the unusual nature of their speech. Comments were made to the effect that their 'language is a new confusion' and that they had a 'dialect and manner peculiar to themselves' (1935, p. 193). Support for the theory is also provided by the existence of a nautical element in all pidgins and creoles with European lexicons. In Cameroon pidgin one finds a set which includes *hib* < 'heave', to push or lift; *jam* < 'jam', to be stalemated; *kapsai* < 'capsize', to overturn or spill; *manawa* < 'man o' war', a wasp. Many similar items occur in other Atlantic pidgins and creoles while the following is a selection from Neo-Melanesian: *haisim* < 'hoist', to raise; *hivim* < 'heave', push, lift; *kapsait* < 'capsize', turn over; and *kapstan* < 'capstan', cut tobacco. It is interesting as well as relevant to this theory that other European-language-based pidgins and creoles also have a nautical set. In Haiti, for example, one finds *hele/rele* < 'heler', to call out, hail; *lage* < 'larguer', let go; *mare* < 'amarrer', to tie; and *rale* < 'haler', to pull or haul.

The nautical jargon theory is an attractive one, but it also fails to explain the many structural affinities that exist between pidgin and creole Englishes and their French, Portuguese, Spanish and Dutch counterparts. It is its ability to do just that which is the main attraction of the monogenetic or relexification theory.

The monogenetic/relexification theory

According to this theory all European-language-based pidgins and creoles derive from a fifteenth-century Portuguese pidgin. In turn, this was probably a relic of the medieval *Lingua Franca* (also called Sabir) which was the common auxiliary language of the multilingual Crusaders and of Mediterranean traders. Records show that Lingua Franca differed in vocabulary from area to area but its structure seems to have been relatively static and bears some resemblance to modern pidgins and creoles. The following extract from Molière's *Le Bourgeois Gentilhomme* (IV, 5, 1971 edn, pp. 769–70) is a literary re-creation of Lingua Franca but it clearly illustrates the reduction in pronominal forms, 'ti' instead of 'tu/te' and also the use of an invariable verb form:

Se ti sabir,	(if you know
Ti respondir;	you reply

Se non sabir	if you don't know
Tazir, tazir.	be quiet, be quiet.
Mi star Mufti:	I am Mufti:
Ti qui star ci?	Who are you?
Non intendir:	if you don't hear
Tazir, tazir.	be quiet, be quiet.)

An 1830 account of the Algerian version of Lingua Franca also contains examples of features frequently associated with pidgins. In this case, the vocabulary is taken largely from Italian. As in the extract from Molière it uses *star* as an unchanging *BE* verb and, in addition, it contains examples of reduplication like *poco poco ablar per ti* (you speak too little)

Table 11

Lingua Franca	English
qui star aki?	who is there?
intrar	come in
oundé ti vénir?	where do you come from?
ové ti andar?	where are you going?
mi andar spasségiar	I am going for a stroll
ti quérir mi andar con ti?	do you want me to go with you?
si, andar siémé siémé	yes, let's go together

(p. 96). In the 1830 examples the negator occurs in the same position as in the pidgins and creoles we have examined, *qouesto non star vero* (that's not true) (p. 93) and it tends to use an unmarked verb form (p. 95; see Table 11).

Those who support the monogenetic theory of pidginization believe that when the Portuguese sailed along the west coast of Africa in the fifteenth century they would, naturally, have used their Mediterranean contact language, their Portuguese form of Sabir. This would have been the first European language that the Africans acquired. Then, in the sixteenth and seventeenth centuries, as Portuguese influence in Africa waned and as the pidgin was used in more and more contact situations, pidgin speakers drew on the dominant language in the area for vocabulary expansion. In different areas and at different times the dominant language may have been English or Spanish, French or Dutch. The Portuguese were also among the first European traders in India and the Far East, and so a Portuguese pidgin could also have been the model for China coast pidgin English and its modern offshoots, Beach-la-Mar and Neo-Melanesian. According to this theory one should think in terms of an anglicized pidgin Portuguese or a gallicized pidgin Portuguese rather than a pidgin English or a pidgin French.

One can find textual references to both Lingua Franca and 'bastard Portuguese' along the African coast and in the East, references which give considerable support to the theory. Barbot offered the following advice to travellers going to 'Guinea and the American islands, especially if they were never there before . . . In the first place it is requisite for the person that designs to travel into those parts to learn languages, as English, French, Low Dutch, Portuguese and Lingua Franca' (1746, vol. 5, p. 11). Phillips travelled along the West African coast in 1693–4 and commented thus on people he met in Cabo Corce castle: 'The next to him was a Mr. William Ronan, an Irish gentleman, who had lived long in France, and spake that language fluently, as well as the bastard Portuguese the negroes use along this coast' (1746, vol. 6, p. 220). With regard to the East, Jespersen draws attention to Noble's eighteenth-century description of the Chinese who spoke a 'broken and mixed dialect of English and Portuguese' (1922, p. 222).

Apart from the textual references to the widespread nature of an early Portuguese-based trade language, lexical and syntactic similarities can be shown to exist between present-day Portuguese pidgins and creoles and those related to other European languages. Vocabulary items deriving ultimately from Portuguese and occurring in all pidgin and creole Englishes have already been referred to, items like *savi/sabi*, *pikin/pikinini*, and the structural similarities may be illustrated from the Portuguese creole of Guiné and Krio, the English-based creole of Sierra Leone (see Table 12). It is instructive to compare the final sentence with the Portuguese equivalent, 'está na casa', and notice that *na* appears in all three. When the same structural form, in this case 'na', appears in different languages with approximately the same meaning, one may assume that the similarity is due either to chance or to a relationship between the languages. Taylor (1971, p. 294) draws attention to twelve such structural markers which occur in a large number of European-language-based pidgins and

Table 12

English	Crioulo/Portuguese creole	Krio
it is very nice (lit. he nice too much)	*i saabi dɔmaas*	*i fain tumɔs*
come/you (pl) come	*naa/ali naa*	*kam/una kam*
he doesn't know anything (lit. he no know nothing)	*i ka sibi naada*	*i nɔ sabi nating*
he is at home (lit. he be in house)	*i staa na kaasa*	*i de na ɔs*

creoles. Such a high incidence of structural similarities would seem to rule out chance as the explanation.

The monogenetic theory gains further support from the realization that attested examples of relexification, that is the replacement of the lexicon of one stock by the lexicon of another, can be cited. Saramaccan, for example, while regarded as an English creole, has a large Portuguese element in its vocabulary in that approximately 30 per cent can be traced directly to Portuguese. One can make a good case, historical as well as linguistic, that in Saramaccan we have a creole that was originally Portuguese-based but which, because of being cut off from the influence of English in 1667 when England ceded Surinam to Holland, had not completed the process of relexification. But it is not only in the remote past that one finds examples of the relexification process. Wurm describes how the English-based Beach-la-Mar was ousted from New

Caledonia after 1853 when French became the official language of the island. A French pidgin gradually developed which 'had its origin in the gradual relexification of Beach-la-Mar, and for a long time, appears to have displayed in its vocabulary a mixture of English, French and native words' (1971, p. 1006).

At this stage it may be of value to examine in somewhat closer detail the linguistic changes involved in the process of relexification. Assuming, for the moment, that in a particular area of West Africa a Portuguese pidgin was the most widely used auxiliary language in the early seventeenth century, as England's interest in the area increased, the English eased the Portuguese from their position of mercantile and political pre-eminence. At first, in order to communicate with the Africans

Table 13

English	from Portuguese	from English
know	*sabi*	*no*
basket	*blai*	*baskit*
baby	*pikin*	*bebi*

in the area, some of the English would have been obliged to learn the Portuguese pidgin; but, in time, English words would also be used and doublets might appear in the language, one item from Portuguese, the other from English. This stage of language blend might well be described as a 'broken and mixed dialect of English and Portuguese' (Jespersen, 1922, p. 222). If contact with English continued, the English lexicon would eventually replace the Portuguese, which might only leave a few relics in the 'new' pidgin; and thus the process of relexification would be complete, as it may be in Krio from which the above doublets are taken. When a pidgin reached this stage it would continue to look to the dominant language, in this case English, as and when new lexical items were required.

It is quite possible that relexification did occur and on quite a large scale, though it is not easy to explain why a people who already possessed a satisfactory core vocabulary would give it up. Paradoxically, the relexification theory would probably be more acceptable if it had been *less* successful; if it had, in other words, left larger traces of the original pidgin, particularly in terms of core vocabulary. Yet this would be only a minor snag if one could adopt the position of Dalby who, in referring to West African languages (1970a, p. 6), claims that their multiplicity

> relates particularly to the individual vocabularies of African languages. Divergences in their structures, i.e. in their grammatical, phonological and semantic systems, are frequently less extensive than their divergences of vocabulary, and— relative to the structures of European languages—West African languages are found to share many widespread structural features. As a result, Africans are often well experienced in operating divergent sets of vocabulary, as they master a variety of local languages, but in doing so are able to maintain many of the grammatical, phonological and semantic rules which they have acquired as part of their original mother tongue.

Assuming that Dalby's position is tenable, it would therefore have been a relatively familiar task for the West African to acquire first of all a Portuguese vocabulary to be wielded like any other lexical set at his disposal, and which might be discarded in favour of some other set from another European language if and when the need arose. Such an explanation would certainly account for the syntactic similarities in Atlantic pidgins and creoles, though it would mean rewriting the relexification theory, making an African substratum rather than a Portuguese pidgin the syntactic base of today's pidgins and creoles. Even this position was more or less espoused by Sylvain who had this to say of Haitian creole in 1936: 'Nous sommes en présence d'un français coulé dans le moule de la syntaxe africaine ou, comme on classe généralement les langues d'après leur parenté syntaxique, d'une langue éwé à vocabulaire français.' ('We are in the presence of a French which has been cast in the mould of an African syntax or, since languages are generally classified according to their syntactic ancestry, in the presence of an Ewe language with a

French vocabulary', p. 178.) Most creolists would now regard Sylvain's as an extreme claim and besides, to sidestep a pidgin Portuguese is to lose the advantage that it offers in explaining the structural similarities in all European-language-based pidgins and creoles and not only those with a West African connection.

The monogenetic theory, envisaging a Portuguese pidgin, deriving ultimately from Sabir, as the originator of both Atlantic and Pacific pidgins and creoles through a process of relexification, has many attractions, most notably its comprehensiveness; but the case for this theory, as for the others considered, calls for a verdict of 'not proven'. What is clear is that pidgins, by shedding linguistic redundancies, by adopting greater syntactic regularity, by jettisoning linguistic inessentials, have very successfully eradicated the very features which would allow linguists to link them, unequivocally, with a particular language or family of languages. (Figure 1 shows the suggested derivation of the world-wide network of European-language-based pidgins and creoles.)

Its comprehensiveness is the chief merit of the monogenetic theory, and yet it is not comprehensive enough. Other pidgins and creoles exist in the world which are not based on European languages and which yet share some of the characteristics of all the pidgins and creoles so far discussed. In Africa one can find pidgin versions of Ewondo, Hausa, Ngbandi, Zulu, Bemba and Swahili. In Papua a pidginized version of Motu is widely used, especially by the police force and other civil authorities; and a pidginized Malay has widespread currency in Indonesia and Malaysia. Specific examples should more easily highlight the similarities that exist between these pidgins and those related to European languages.

Ewondo Populaire is one of the names given to a pidginized Ewondo spoken in the vicinity of Yaoundé in Cameroon. It came into being, as did the various English pidgins, to facilitate communication in a multilingual area. Alexandre claims that it is not used in isolated areas but is restricted to places where commercial and administrative contacts occur (see 1962, p. 253). Like many pidgins, Ewondo Populaire has a limited

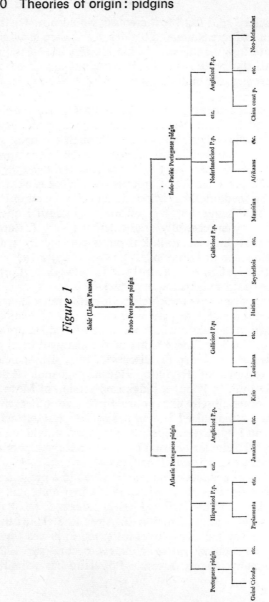

Figure 1

vocabulary which, in Alexandre's opinion, corresponds to the needs of a modern way of life, to 'voyage, commerce, rélations avec les autorités' ('travelling, trading, dealings with the authorities') (p. 254). When compared with Ewondo it is clear that there has been a considerable reduction in inflection and grammatical contrasts, commonly found in Bantu languages (see p. 254). The verb phrase, in particular, is much simpler than in the standard variety of Ewondo and can be meaningfully compared with English-based pidgins and creoles (see Table 14). In standard Ewondo the negator is variable, but in

Table 14

English	Freetown Krio	Ewondo Populaire
I do	*a du*	*me bo*
I don't do	*a nɔ du*	*me kɛ bo*
Do	*du*	*boo*
Don't do	*nɔ du*	*ke boo*
I did	*a bin du*	*me nga bo*
I didn't do	*a nɔ bin du*	*me ke nga bo*

Ewondo Populaire it is invariable and, like the negators in English-based pidgins, it follows the subject and precedes the verb phrase or initiates a negative imperative sentence.

Police Motu has been widely used around Port Moresby for at least a century. Like other pidgins referred to, it has a smaller vocabulary than the language to which it is related, a vocabulary which aims at maximum utility in a contact situation. Motu has several tenses, and a complex system of verbal distinctions all of which are carried by affixes. Police Motu has shed most of the inflectional system and tends to indicate verbal distinctions by means of auxiliaries (see Wurm, 1971, pp. 1010–16).

Ewondo Populaire and Police Motu are like European-language-based pidgins and creoles in that they all tend to discard inflections although inflection is a feature of the languages from which their lexicons are taken. In all of them syntactic relationships tend to be indicated by word order rather than by morphological change, with the result that word order is more rigid and more strictly adhered to than in their non-pidginized counterparts.

Another explanation: a synthesis

The similarities revealed by all pidgins and creoles so far studied and the difficulties encountered in trying to locate their historical origins, suggest that it is, perhaps, shortsighted to look to the past, to look for a 'common' origin in the sense of their being descended from one parent language, or even from a number of languages. Perhaps it would be more profitable to look for a 'common' origin in another sense; that is by examining the possibility that there are universal patterns of linguistic behaviour appropriate to contact situations. One could express this view more positively by suggesting that pidgins and creoles are alike because, fundamentally, languages are alike and simplification processes are alike. Seeing in the structural simplicity of pidgins and creoles a similarity due to inherent universal linguistic constraints precludes the necessity of postulating a proto-pidgin, whether of African, European or any other origin. The similarities in all pidgins from the past as well as the present, and from all continents, may well be accounted for if one can show that human beings are biologically programmed to acquire *Language* rather than any particular language, and that the programming includes an innate ability to dredge one's linguistic behaviour of superficial redundancies where there is a premium on transmitting facts, on communicating, as it were, without frills. It is not being suggested that one is consciously aware of *how* one adjusts one's language behaviour. But the fact that one does adjust and the fact that people of different linguistic backgrounds adjust their language behaviour in similar ways, suggests that the behaviour is rule-governed and may be the result of linguistic universals.

This is a very large claim, but one which has the merit of encompassing all the other theories. It does not insist on the origin of the pidgin phenomena in a particular time or place. It argues that, although some pidgins and creoles are undoubtedly related, others may have grown up independently; since children, sailors, Levantine traders and Portuguese adventurers might all have been responding to linguistic situations according to an innate behavioural 'blueprint'. While one cannot prove such a theory conclusively—after all one is dealing with properties of the mind—one can provide a considerable amount of evidence in support of it.

Both linguists and psychologists are aware of the puzzle posed by the fact that children manage to acquire the grammar of the language or languages of their early environment, in spite of being exposed to only a finite sample of utterances, many of which are not well formed. The exposure to language differs for each child in the community, yet they all acquire approximately the same grammar, and in doing so learn to produce and respond to an infinite variety of novel utterances. When it comes to explaining how a child, at an age when it has scarcely learnt to control its limbs and when its reasoning powers are demonstrably weak, can nevertheless acquire a language, the experts are divided. Behaviourists claim that language learning differs in no fundamental way from any other form of stimulus-controlled behaviour. On the other hand, followers of what one might call the 'Species-Specific' school suggest that human beings are genetically endowed with the ability to acquire language. Of course, much of our language behaviour is 'conditioned' either overtly or covertly. There is certainly an element of reward and punishment, and very high motivation, in language learning in infancy; but the more deeply scholars study language the more the uncovered evidence seems to point towards a genetic basis for its acquisition. A brief review of such evidence will be given because it has a direct bearing on pidginization. If it is possible to show that human beings have predetermined biological propensities for acquiring language then it may well be that the capacity for linguistic simplification and accommodation—the process which produces pidgins—is also innate and universal.

Eric Lenneberg (1964, pp. 65–88) discusses the reasons for

suspecting that language is species-specific, that is, a biologically conditioned human attribute. He draws attention to the fact that there is some correlation between one side of the brain and speech performance. As Carroll puts it (1964, p. 45):

> It is generally agreed that speech functions take place in only one hemisphere of the brain, usually the side of the brain opposite to hand preference; thus the left hemisphere is the 'dominant hemisphere' of most righthanded people. There are cases on record of complete hemispherectomy; if the hemisphere excised controls speech, the patient will not be able to learn or relearn language unless he is still quite young (no more than ten years of age).

The isolation of the 'speech centre', usually in the left hemisphere of the brain, does not prove, but certainly supports, a biological view of language and language learning.

The regularity of the onset and mastery of speech supports such a view. The stages in the development of language seem to be largely unaffected by cultural differences. Children, of all races, first begin to babble, then to acquire the intonational patterns of their speech community, to produce individual words and then short combinations of words. So regular and so apparently automatic is this behaviour that Lenneberg refers to the stages as 'maturational milestones' (p. 66). Significantly, these developmental milestones occur in the same order for all children, even those who are severely subnormal, and if a young child, around three or under, suffers brain damage, his process of recovery often involves his going through the same stages again; first babbling, then using words individually and in combinations. It would therefore appear that these stages are triggered off biologically.

When acquiring language, children produce patterns which are regular for them but irregular when measured against the norms of adult society. In such cases children cannot be said to be imitating adults. Studies in unrelated languages like English, Congolese Luo and Finnish suggest that a child's first negatives are regularly 'Negator plus Sentence', e.g. 'No/not' plus 'I go'. There is a rule here and, since it is not the adult rule, it would appear to be the child's own contribution.

This type of linguistic behaviour seems to reflect an innate urge to impose a pattern on language. Indeed, one can go further and point out that it is almost impossible to *prevent* a child acquiring language. As long as he is exposed to language he will acquire it, often in spite of handicaps like neglect, blindness and even deafness.

The points that have been made above are valid for human beings generally rather than for any particular language group; but in any case, however different cultures may be, or however different languages may appear to be, all human languages are based on principles of sounds, patterns and meaning, that is, phonology, syntax and semantics. In addition, a child will learn the language of his environment irrespective of the culture or society he was born into because the basic skills for language learning appear to be built into man's genetic structure.

One could add to the above theories which tend to underline the non-behaviouristic aspects of language learning. One could also refine on much of the evidence. But they have been presented here, not to prove a psycholinguistic theory so much as to show that it is highly probable that man's ability to use language is the result of certain species-specific biological capacities. One can compare the mastery of speech with the ability to walk. A child begins to stand and take faltering steps at a particular stage in his physical development. He can be encouraged in this but he cannot be 'forced' to walk before he has reached a certain maturational point. The ability to walk on two feet is in his pre-programming, though it may not appear until the child is about a year old. Similarly, given a speaking environment, a child will begin to speak at a certain stage in his development. Many accidents can occur to prevent a child's acquiring speech, however, because just as an acorn is a potential oak tree, not a miniature one, so is a child a potential user of language, born with an innate store of linguistic universals which may, or may not, be developed. What these universals are or what form they take need not be explored further here. Such universals are of relevance only in so far as they shed light on the origin of pidgins. If all humans are born with a biological predisposition to acquire and manipulate language, then it is likely that there are linguistic universals common to all languages, irrespective of their surface manifestations. And it also seems likely from an examination of a variety of contact situations that, at times, a speaker may be able to get access to, or reactivate, these universals, these propensities for coming to terms with linguistic situations.

When Brown and Bellugi examined how children acquired language they discovered that the mother, when talking to the child, almost invariably and without realizing it simplified her speech. Her conversation tended to be of the here and now. In addition, the mother's speech differed from that normally employed by adults in that the sentences were 'short and simple—the kind of sentence Adam [one of the children studied] will produce a year later' (1964, p. 135). A possible generalization from the children studied is that 'a child's introduction to English ordinarily comes in the form of a simplified, repetitive, and idealised dialect' (p. 136); but the point worth dwelling on here is that many parents automatically simplify their language when speaking to very young children. They cut down on sentence subordination, use simple tenses, repeat new words. And they do this without being fully conscious of what they are doing or how they achieve it. In other words, their behaviour seems to respond to a built-in simplification mechanism.

Charles Ferguson goes further. He does not believe that only parents or people dealing with children have a simple 'register' or 'mode of speech appropriate for use with particular statuses, roles or situations' (1971, p. 143). In his opinion, 'many, perhaps all, speech communities have registers of a special kind for use with people who are regarded for one reason or another as being unable readily to understand the normal speech of the community (e.g. babies, foreigners, deaf people)' (p. 143). Ferguson has found that where inflection exists in the 'full' language, it tends to be discarded in the 'simple' register. The examples from English, French and Spanish in Table 15 support such a belief and also suggest that languages tend to simplify in similar ways. Further research is needed before one can state categorically that *all* languages have a simple register but the concept is not limited to Indo-European languages. Lamso, in Cameroon, has a vocabulary set, containing several reduplicated forms, which is employed to and by children with whom also tonal contrasts are kept to a minimum. It is a stimulating thought that pidgins may result from such 'simple' exchanges. Babies soon discard the simple

Table 15

	full language	simple register
English	Your daddy has gone away.	Daddy gone
French	Ton papa est parti.	Papa parti
English	I see the soldier.	Me see soldier
Spanish	Yo veo al soldado.	Me ver soldado

'idealized dialect' because social pressures put a premium on their acquiring the language of the adult community. But such pressure did not, in the past, prevail in pidgin situations and so the urge to modify towards a more 'acceptable' norm was not a factor in the formation of pidgins.

Additional support is given to the suggestion that, on occasion, all speakers can utilize a 'simple register' by Roman Jakobson, who points out (1968, pp. 16–17) that:

> It has been established repeatedly that a child in full control of his language can suddenly take pleasure in reverting to the role of a baby and, either by imitating a younger brother or sister, or to some extent through his own recollection, attempt once more to talk like one. To a different degree, the infantile instinct may also appear in adult life, as psychoanalysis in particular has stressed. And Gabelentz has pointed out that courting lovers quite frequently talk in child language.

It is the latter part of the quotation that relates to the present argument, though it is significant that an adult can, under certain conditions, revert to babbling, the earliest overt manifestation of language. The above evidence suggests that lovers may be added to the list of speakers who can, when the need arises, use a simplified version of their normal language. Nor is our list even now complete. The writer of the 'Battle of Harlaw' uses the same simplifying techniques to distinguish between the speech of a Gaelic speaker and a Scot (Child, 1962 edn, vol. 3, Ballad No. 163):

As I cam in by Dunidier
An doun by Netherha,
There was fifty thousand Hielanmen
A-marching to Harlaw.

As I cam on, an farther on,
An doun an by Balquhain,
Oh there I met Sir James the Rose,
Wi him Sir John the Gryme.

'O cam ye frae the Hielans, man?
An cam ye a' the wey?
Saw ye MacDonell an his men,
As they cam frae the Skee?'

'Yes, me cam frae ta Hielans, man,
An me cam a' ta wey,
An she saw MacDonell an his men,
As they cam frae ta Skee.'

'Oh was ye near MacDonell's men?
Did ye their numbers see?
Come, tell to me, John Hielanman,
What micht their numbers be?'

'Yes, me was near, an near eneuch,
An me their numbers saw;
There was fifty thousan Heilanmen
A-marchin to Harlaw.'

A reference to a Scottish ballad may seem a far cry from the origin of pidgins, but in it we see some language use which relates directly to the present argument. In particular, the Gaelic speaker uses 'me cam' for the Scots 'I cam', 'ta Hielans' instead of 'the Hielans' and 'she saw MacDonell an his men' where there seems to be a confusion of pronouns. All these features, the use of 'me' for 'I', the replacing of /θ, ð/ by /t, d/ and the simplification and/or confusion of pronouns, occur widely in English-based pidgins and creoles. It is not being suggested that the Highlander spoke pidgin Scots; but in this ballad we have an attempt to show how a Gaelic speaker's Scots differed from the standard form. Whether it is an accurate portrayal or merely the opinion of the poet is not important. It seems to add further support to the view that there is a common core English which can be utilized in language contact situations.

This last theory is the simplest and the most adequate partly because it comprehends all the others; but perhaps it is short-sighted to insist on the absolute authority of any one theory. I have no doubt that in certain places at certain times English speakers did talk to the people they came into contact with as if they were children, and as if they would not understand the full language; that sailors were not averse to sharing their nautical jargon with the people whose way of life they shared, often for months at a time; that relexification did occur and that, at the same time, a universal process of simplification was at work. The exact details of origin and development of pidgins can be guessed at but never known with absolute certainty. As Krio says: *dɔg drim lɛf na im bɛlɛ* (dog dream leave in he belly) —'a dog's dream remains in his heart'; in other words, there are some truths we can never uncover.

Chapter four

The process of development: from pidgin to creole

if a no pas sliv a pas pɔkɛt (if I no pass sleeve I pass pocket), i.e. I have strong points as well as weaknesses.

Originally, by very definition, all pidgins were restricted with regard to user and use. In the early stages they would have had small vocabularies and few syntactic rules; they would have been capable of dealing with only a limited range of subjects, with commands, yes/no questions, and with the simplest of explanations. They would have utilized gesture to reinforce or clarify meanings and they would have proved inadequate for sustained conversation. From these origins they developed either as extended pidgins or as creoles and became capable of expressing the views and beliefs of their users, became capable of permitting intergroup communication in areas where it had not existed before, became capable of sustaining a considerable literature. How did this happen?

Although the process of pidginization is not limited to such areas, it seems likely that extended pidgins and creoles develop only in multilingual areas. Where the contact is between two languages only, one or both groups acquire the other language, either keeping or relinquishing their own in the process. But in a multilingual area, a lingua franca, accessible to all groups, is essential if viable and mutual communication is to occur. Once even the most rudimentary form of English developed in, say, West Africa, it would have been used by sailors, traders and settlers to the Africans they contacted and especially to their African wives and concubines. Presumably, some of the children of such unions would have been bilingual in the mother's language and in the pidgin spoken by the parents to each other. It would also have been used by African to African when they spoke mutually unintelligible languages. At first this would only have happened when Africans were brought as slaves from different regions and kept at the ports while the ships were prepared for the journey to the New World. Naturally, the slaves communicated with each other on board ship and more especially while living and working on plantations. It is likely that the use of the pidgin in domestic and slave situations was a vital factor in its expansion because, in such situations, the pidgin was the only available lingua franca and thus had to be developed to serve a wider range of communication needs than were required for simple barter. Continuing to focus attention on English-based languages, four main phases in the expansion process can be distinguished. Phase 1 would have involved casual and unsustained contact between English speakers and the local people. From such contact a marginal pidgin evolves; capable, with the help of gestures, of communicating needs, numbers, trading arrangements, etc. Phase 2 would have begun as soon as the pidgin English was used by and between local people. At this stage it could be expanded in only one way, from the users' mother tongues. This phase helps to account for the indigenous lexical items and the numerous direct translations found in all pidgin and creole Englishes. As inter-racial contact increased phase 3 occurred. At this time vocabularies were extended by borrowing lexical items from the 'dominant' language. Usually, as in Hawaii and Sierra Leone, this language was English, but occasionally, as in Surinam, it was another European language, Dutch in the case of Surinam. Phase 4 is limited to areas where English continued to be an official state language. When the contact between English and the related pidgin or creole was sustained and as education in standard English became more widespread, a process of decreolization occurred. The pidgin/creole became more and more influenced by the standard in phonology, lexis and syntax until one found, and finds, 'a considerable range of English . . . from the home-grown pidgins and creoles at one end of the spectrum to the universally accepted formal written registers of standard English' (Spencer, 1971, p. 6). Evidence for such a continuum is to be found in the West Indies, in West Africa, in Hawaii, in parts of Papua New Guinea and indeed in all anglophone areas of the world where a creole or extended pidgin is an important lingua franca. Some students of American 'black English', like Dillard (1972), have argued that the English of black Americans should be viewed, not as substandard white English, descended from the English spoken on the *Mayflower*, but a related language descended from a variety of creole English spoken by African slaves throughout the West Indies and the southern states of North America. If such a theory can be sustained it will have profoundly important implications for the teaching of English in these areas and to black Americans generally.

The useful term applied to the spectrum that can exist between a creole and a standard form of English is 'post-creole continuum'. If one takes the Jamaican situation to represent such a continuum one finds no clearly defined dividing line between the 'pure' creole and a Jamaican standard. The postulated 'pure' creole described by Bailey (1966) is as much an idealization as 'the English language'. It is a quintessential creole to be found in no one person's speech repertoire, but it is a necessary yardstick for measuring all varieties of Jamaican English. The end points of the Jamaican continuum are mutually unintelligible, but there is no clear cut-off point where the creole ends and the standard begins. In this way a post-creole continuum resembles a dialect/standard spectrum, the difference being one of degree rather than essence, in the sense that it is not usual to find a dialect of English which is mutually unintelligible with the local standard.

The 'post-creole continuum' concept is of value too in allowing the linguist to distinguish between areas like Surinam where the three English creoles, Sranan, Saramaccan and Djuka, have not been exposed to the influence of English since the seventeenth century, with the exception of two minor periods totalling fifteen years, and where there is a distinct cut-off point between English and the creoles, and an area like Freetown where, as early as 1962, Berry drew attention to the co-existence of at least three types of related Englishes between the two officially recognized end points, English and Krio (p. 221).

A more detailed analysis follows of the stages in the creolization process, a process illustrated from both the Atlantic and the Pacific areas.

Phase 1   *Marginal contact*

Hall has pointed out that 'pidgin languages can be found at all social levels and in all kinds of situations' (1966, p. xii). Guides often simplify their language when showing foreign visitors around; so too do English youth hostellers simplify their English when dealing with other hostellers whose command of English is limited. Chapter 3 has suggested that there may well be a universal method of simplifying one's language, an intuitive means of using basic structures. Whatever the validity of such a theory, the English-speaking sailors, traders and adventurers who first went to Africa, Asia, America or Australia must have used a simplified and limited form of English in order to communicate. Such marginal communication soon proves unsatisfactory, and very early attempts were made to train interpreters in England. The Leigh expedition to South America in 1605 found in the Oyapock region Indians 'which had been before in England, and could speak some English' (Purchas, 1625, p. 1250); and there were so many Africans in England as early as 1596 that Elizabeth sent a letter to the Lord Mayors of London and other cities claiming that 'there are of late divers blackamoors brought into these realms, of which kind there are already here to manie, considerynge how God had blessed this land with great increase of people' (Acts of the Privy Council, 26, 1596–7, p. 16). A marginal pidgin is inadequate for more than the most rudimentary forms of communication. Since it is largely supplemented by gesture discussion is limited to tangible objects, especially those in the immediate vicinity. Such a mode of communication is of limited value only. If the contact is prolonged and intimate a fuller form of communication must develop and the pidgin either abandoned or expanded. It is likely that since the sixteenth century several pidgin Englishes have come into existence and died out. Reference has already been made to the English-based Beach-la-Mar being replaced by a French

P C—E

pidgin in New Caledonia (ch. 3) and Korean Bamboo English is already almost extinct since it is no longer a necessary aid to communication in Korea. The only two options open to a marginal pidgin is to disappear or to become more useful by the expansion of its resources.

Phase 2   Period of nativization

The expansion of a pidgin is facilitated by two main factors: its developing in a multilingual area and its use not so much in non-native to native contact as in contacts between native inhabitants speaking mutually unintelligible languages. It is theoretically possible that pidgin English could be expanded in English-to-native contact situations; in this case, however, it is likely that the marginal pidgin would become more and more like the form of English used by the English speakers in the contact situation. In the Atlantic as well as the Pacific the two factors operated. In West Africa, as in PNG, a pidgin was vitally important in bridging linguistic barriers between the peoples native to these areas. In both areas it was expanded because of its local usefulness. If and when such expanded pidgins become more widely used as first languages it will be from choice, not necessity as it was in the West Indies where slaves, taken from many parts of West Africa, were compelled by circumstances to adopt the pidgin as their one effective means of intercommunication. The expansion of a pidgin may be seen in all three areas, but in West Africa and PNG speakers had and have little need to abandon their local vernaculars.

Initially, as we have seen, a pidgin is inadequate for the expression of a very wide range of human experience. As it becomes more widely used its vocabulary is increased, and as its vocabulary increases it becomes more useful. Let us briefly examine the position of an African or a Papuan who had acquired a restricted pidgin. As with other learners of a new language they must frequently have encountered objects or concepts for which they had no name in the new language. In the usual learning situation the learner can ask for the word, but that course was usually not open to restricted pidgin speakers. In such circumstances they could use a reduplicated form, though this might not always be feasible or meaningful; they could use a word or phrase from their mother tongue, though if this practice were over-indulged it could lessen the value of the lingua franca in intergroup communication. If these two methods proved abortive they could use a 'calque', a type of loan translation using the word resources of the pidgin in a direct translation from the vernaculars. All these methods were indeed utilized and they are largely responsible for giving the different pidgins and creoles their individual character.

Reduplications Reduplicated forms occur in all the English-based pidgins and creoles. Besides reduplications taken over from the local languages, three types of reduplicated English forms can be attested (see Table 16): (a) reduplications to reduce the number of homophonous forms; (b) reduplications which extend the meaning of the simple form, and (c) reduplications

Table 16

	Atlantic		Pacific	
(a)	*san*	—sun	*pis*	—peace
	sansan	—sand	*pispis*	—urinate
	was	—wash	*sip*	—ship
	waswas	—wasp	*sipsip*	—sheep
(b)	*ben*	—bend	*sing*	—sing
	benben	—crooked	*singsing*	—ritual singing
	wan	—one	*was*	—wash
	wanwan	—one by one	*waswas*	—go to wash
(c)	*kɔs*	—curse	*luk*	—look
	kɔskɔs	—curse again and again	*lukluk*	—stare at, see
	krai	—cry	*tɔk*	—talk
	kraikrai	—cry continuously	*tɔktɔk*	—chatter
	fain	—lovely	*bik*	—big
	fainfain	—very lovely	*bikbik*	—huge, very big

used as intensives, this type being confined to the adjective/ verb class.

Items borrowed from indigenous languages The lexical items which found their way from local languages into pidgin and creole Englishes were often, not unexpectedly, related to the local culture and conditions, as the examples in Table 17 suggest.

Table 17

Atlantic		Pacific	
akara	—beancake	*balus*	—bird, pigeon
mboma	—boaconstrictor	*kapul*	—tree kangaroo
mukala	—whiteman	*kiau*	—egg
ngɔmbi	—spirit	*mbambu*	—mother's brother's son
kɔnggɔsa	—gossip	*ngambwa*	—spirit

Word-compounding and calquing To extend the pidgin's vocabulary one could combine different items from the pidgin either (a) on the analogy of English patterns, or (b) in direct translations from the mother tongues, as in Table 18. It is a reasonable hypothesis that lexical expansion was accompanied by a growth in the pidgin's ability to mark grammatical distinctions overtly. As the vocabulary was expanded the pidgin became more useful in a wider set of communication exchanges but its greater usefulness also presupposed finer syntactic and semantic distinctions. With regard to the Atlantic pidgins and creoles it seems likely that these finer distinctions may have been introduced in phase 2 because they appear to reflect African mother-tongue influence as the comparison in Table 19 indicates. One must not, however, assume that every feature of a pidgin or a creole can be related directly to any of the parent languages. As was mentioned in the Introduction, pidgins, in expanding, evolve lexical items and linguis-

Table 18

Atlantic		Pacific	
(a) *bigman*	—(<big+man) important person	*bigsɔnde*	—(<big+Sunday) feastday [adj.+n.]
bushbif	—(<bush+beef) wild animal, game	*bushnaif*	—(<bush+knife) strong knife [n.+a.]
daiman	—(<die+man) corpse	*daiman*	—(<die+man) corpse [v.+n.]
(b) *bigai*	—(<big+eye) greed, greedy	*bigmaus*	—(<big+mouth) conceited
draiskin	—(<dry+skin) thin	*draibon*	—(<dry+bone) tough
mamiwata	—(<mammy+water) female water spirit	*klaudibrok*	—(<cloud+broke) thunder, cloudburst
switmɔt	—(<sweet+mouth) flatter, flattery	*smɔlmama*	—(<small+mama) aunt, female relative
taifes	—(<tie+face) frown	*wanlain*	—(<one+line) of the same age group

Table 19

English	Cameroon pidgin	Lamso
go	*go*	duh
she goes to market	*i go maket*	wu duh wai
she is going to market	*i di go maket*	wu si duh wai
is she going to market?	*i di go maket?*	wu si duh wai?
she went to market	*i bin go maket*	wu u duh wai
she has (just now) gone to market	*i dɔng go maket* (*naunau*)	wu ki duh wai (lenlen)
she will go to market	*i go go maket*	wu yi duh wai

tic characteristics unique to themselves. Just as, on the lexical plane, for example, a compound like 'washman' for a man employed to do washing is not derived directly from English or any of the African languages; so, on the syntactic plane, a sentence like *no bi na so i dei*—'that's not how it is', while perfectly acceptable in Cameroon pidgin, has no close parallel in either the vernaculars or English.

Phase 3 Influence from the dominant language

When a pidgin has evolved to phase 2 it is capable of being used as a mother tongue and it is from this point in development that it becomes hard, if not impossible, to distinguish between pidgins and creoles by purely linguistic criteria. As the usefulness of the pidgin grows and as its functions extend the lexicon increases and the syntactic properties are refined. The pidgin's expansion is normally closely associated with the 'dominant' language, by which I mean the language of government and education, and this, in turn, is almost always the language from which the pidgin's basic vocabulary is derived. But since this is not inevitably the case two types of influence on the now well-established pidgin can be postulated. Focusing on English-based pidgins again one has the situation where there is influence from the prestigious English causing modification towards the local standard in pronunciation, lexis and, to a lesser extent, syntax; and influence from a prestige language other than English. In the second situation, where English contact has been removed, the pidgin or creole only continues to exist if it was well established when contact with English was withdrawn, and also if it was vitally important as a means of communication. In such circumstances it may continue to expand using its own resources or, more likely, it may borrow from the new dominant language. The Surinamese creoles typify the second case. In Surinam there are three creole Englishes, Sranan, Saramaccan and Djuka, although Surinam was ceded to the Netherlands in 1667. These creoles must have reached phase 2, at least, before then, and continued to exist because their speakers had no other language in common. The coastal creole, Sranan, has had closest contact with Dutch and has therefore been, as one would expect, influenced by Dutch with regard to pronunciation and vocabulary, often passing on the adopted features to the creoles of the interior, Saramaccan and Djuka. A closer comparison of English-dominated with non-English-dominated pidgins and creoles shows that the processes, though similar in cause, are very different in result. Where English has continued to co-exist alongside an English-based pidgin or creole one finds, today, a spectrum of Englishes; where English ceased to influence the language one finds, as in Surinam, that the creole and standard English are completely discrete.

Dominant language: English Cameroon pidgin is a fairly typical example of an extended English-based pidgin which continues to co-exist with standard English and on which therefore English continues to exert an influence. In the pidgin there are clear indications of different periods of borrowing (see Table 20). The early set goes back to a time when the phono-

Table 20

Early	More recent
kwis <squeeze—squeeze	*skwia* <square—square, rectangle
tik <stick —tree, stick, guava	*stia* <stair —staircase, storey
trɔng <strong —strong, be strong, strength	*straik* <strike —strike, stoppage of work

logical structure of the pidgin did not permit consonant clusters beginning with 's'. Different periods of borrowing are also reflected in the existence of lexical pairs which are sometimes slightly differentiated with regard to meaning (see Table 21). The influence of English, especially on the vocabularies of English-based pidgins and creoles, is all-pervasive and a source of almost limitless enrichment. Jones was referring to his own creole when he claimed 'the whole vocabulary of English is potentially Krio' (1971, p. 66) but his remark is applicable to all other pidgins and creoles which co-exist with English, a point underlined by a sentence recorded in Cameroon in 1972, *i bin anaialetam?*, 'did he annihilate them?'

Once a pidgin's grammar is firmly established and can function adequately in any given circumstance, it is less open to change than the pronunciation and the vocabulary, but it too is influenced if the pressures from English endure and persist. In

Table 21

Early		More recent
dres <dress (verb, military)—move, move up—*muf*		
finggafut <finger foot	—toe	—*to*
fokɔna <four corner	—crossroads	—*krɔsrod*
kapsai <capsize	—spill	—*spil*
kɔmbi <company	—friend	—*fren*
manhan <man hand	—right	—*rait*
womanhan <woman hand	—left	—*lef*

the past it is likely that there were two BE-verbs in Cameroon pidgin, a locative verb realized as *dei*, 'there', and an equative verb *na* (etymology uncertain) (Todd, 1973, pp. 1–15; see Table 22). Under the influence of English 'be' Cameroon pidgin

Table 22

Early		More recent
i go dei dei	—he will be there	—*i go bi dei*
i bin dei fɔ haus	—he was in the house	—*i bin bi fɔ haus*
meri na ma sista	—Mary is my sister	—*meri bi ma sista*
yu na hu?	—you are who?	—*yu bi hu?*

can now also use *bi* in both locative and equative sentences. A similar influence can be observed in the use of *beta* as well as *gud pas* for 'better': *i gud pas yu? na so, i beta*, 'is he better than you? That's so, he's better'; and indeed in all areas where the syntax of pidgin differs markedly from the syntax of English.

Dominant language: not English   The continued existence of an English-based pidgin or creole in a situation in which the dominant language is not English is comparatively rare, though it can be found in many of the ports of francophone West Africa and, most clearly, in Surinam. The Surinam creoles must have been stabilized some time before 1667 because not only did they resist wholesale relexification towards Dutch but they also have many structural and lexical affinities with other Atlantic creoles with which they have had little or no contact since the seventeenth century. This can be shown by comparing vocabulary items in Freetown Krio with those in the three Surinam creoles (see Table 23). Nevertheless, as might be

Table 23

English	Krio	Sranan	Djuka	Saramaccan
big	*big*	*bigi*	*bigi*	*bigi*
boaconstrictor	*boma*	*aboma*	*aboma*	*boma*
breast	*bɔbi*	*bɔbi*	*bɔbi*	*bɔbi*
come	*kam*	*kɔm*	*kɔm*	*kõ*
earth	*grɔng*	*grɔng*	*gɔrɔng*	*goon*
remember	*mɛmba*	*memre*	*membe*	*mɛmbɛ*

expected, Dutch has influenced the vocabularies. Often because English and Dutch are closely related languages it is hard to say whether an item derives from English or Dutch or, indeed, whether the similarity of forms has reinforced the creole word (see Table 24). Other items are more easily placed. Sranan's *hansɔn* from English 'handsome' has been almost entirely replaced by Dutch 'mooi' in the form of *mɔi*—'handsome, fine'. Occasionally, Dutch has influenced one of the creoles only; or the English and Dutch borrowings may co-exist; or there may be terms which occur only in the Dutch form, either because the Dutch word has replaced the

Table 24

English	Sranan	Djuka	Saramaccan	Dutch
all	*ala*	*ala*	*tuu/ala*	alle
cold	*koru*	*koo*	*kɔtɔ*	koud
day	*dei*	*dei*	*daka*	dag
five	*feifi*	*feifi*	*feifi*	vijf
green	*grun*	*guun*	*guun/giin*	groen
salt	*sotu*	*sautu*	*satu*	zout
scratch (dial. 'scrab')	*krabu*	*kaabu*	*kaabu*	krab (ben)
wind	*winti*	*winti*	*ventu*	wind

Table 25

English	Sranan	Djuka	Saramaccan	Dutch
dirty	*dɔti/mɔrsu*	*dɔti*	*dɔti*	mors(ig)
teeth	*tifi*	*tifi*	*tanda*	tand
woman	*uma/fro*	*uman*	*muyee* <Port. 'mulher'	vrou
cloud	*wɔrku*	*wɔluku*	*wɔluku*	wolk
flower	*brɔmki*	*bɔɔmiki*	*fɔlɔ* <Port. 'flor'	blommetje
mountain	*bergi*	*beligi*	*kukuna* <Port. 'collina'	berg
sew	*nai*	*nai*	*nai*	naai
write	*skifi*	*sikiifi*	*sikifi*	schrijven

English one or because the concept was only recently introduced into the creoles. All three types of influence are illustrated in Table 25.

Besides the lexical influences Dutch has also exerted slight pressure on pronunciation and on syntax. The influence on pronunciation is usually limited to the borrowing of sounds which would not normally occur in the creoles, as in the Dutch pronunciation of 'gulle', guilder, when the creoles would normally use the form *kole*. With regard to syntax, Sranan, like other pidgins and creoles, has an invariable noun form. Dutch, on the other hand, indicates plurality in the noun and there is a slight tendency for overt plurality marking to occur in the noun in Sranan (Eersel, 1971, pp. 317–22). Dutch has certainly affected the English-based creoles, as the above examples suggest, but the influence has been superficial and the creoles are much more closely related to other Atlantic pidgins and creoles than they are to Dutch, or than they are to the Dutch creole of the Virgin Islands. What marks the Surinam creoles out from the other English-based Atlantic varieties is the fact that, in Surinam, there is a clear demarcation line between the creoles and the official language, and between the creoles and English.

Phase 4   The post-creole continuum

When it is remembered that most extended pidgin and creole Englishes have been in contact with some form of non-creole English for over three hundred years it is not surprising that they have been influenced to varying degrees by the prestigious standard; though it may be only in the recent past, with the introduction of formal education and the spread of literacy in English, that the influences have really begun to make inroads. That the influence could have been a two-way traffic is dealt with later. The process of decreolization is most in evidence in the New World varieties, though it is to be found in all areas where the two types of language co-exist. As education through English was made compulsory in the West Indies long before such a policy was pursued in West Africa or even in urban areas of Papua New Guinea, it is to be expected that decreolization has proceeded furthest in the former area, and that its creoles have absorbed more and more features of standard English.

The post-creole continuum situation may be illustrated by reference to Jamaica, where, between the 'pure' creole described by Bailey (1966) and the standard Jamaican English, which is on a par with all other international forms of standard English, there is a wide range of varieties of English, some nearer the creole end of the spectrum, some nearer the standard end. The two end points are mutually unintelligible but there is no break in the spectrum, and most Jamaicans are adept at manipulating several adjacent varieties of the continuum. There is some correlation between age, education, social status and the section of the spectrum that Jamaicans can command, but rigid correlations cannot be drawn. Craig (1971, pp. 371–91) discovered, for example, that although very young schoolboys may speak reasonably standard English, as they grow older they often adopt many creole features into their speech. This is partly because, with some, the creole is identified with manliness and partly because it can function as a badge of in-group identity. Table 26, giving three sentences

Table 26

English	Intermediate stages	Creole
it's my book	*iz mai buk* *iz mi buk* *a mi buk dat*	*a fi mi buk dat*
where is it?	*wier it iz?* *wier i de?* *we i de?*	*a we i de?*
I didn't eat any	*ai didn it non* *a in nyam non* *mi in nyam non*	*mi na bin nyam non*

from postulated midpoints as well as the two end points on the continuum, indicates some of the possibilities, though many other intermediate realizations have been omitted. And besides such omission, Table 26 gives no indication of the range of possible intonations. The effects of Jamaican creole on a speaker's English may be seen in pronunciation, intonation patterns, lexical selection and sentence structure. And these influences may appear singly or in different combinations. It is true that certain lexical items clearly mark the form of language being used; *nyam*, for example, meaning 'eat', occurs only in the speech of creole speakers or in the English of those who have been strongly influenced by the creole. It is, as it were, a shibboleth of standard Jamaican English. Unfortunately, for the linguist, very few items are so easily and accurately placed. With most words only a context can show clearly the part of the spectrum they belong to.

Having looked at the four hypothetical phases of a pidgin's development a logical question arises. What next? Rather than theorize about abstract possibilities let us consider the variety of English which has been called, among other things, Negro Non-Standard English (NNE), Black English, Negro American English. NNE is the abbreviation currently in vogue and I shall use it to refer to the form of English spoken mainly by black Americans and by the poor whites of the southern states, a form of English which has, until recently, been measured against the American standard and found to be different (if the researcher is sympathetic), deviant (if he insists on using a rigid, normative yardstick) or deficient (if a non-objective viewpoint is adopted). In the main, American dialectologists have sought to explain the differences between NNE and both standard American English and most varieties of non-standard white English by referring to a variety of British dialects and by stressing the social and cultural conditions of NNE speakers, conditions in which non-standard forms might develop and be maintained. Only after Turner (1949) was the African contribution to NNE seriously considered. Turner's book dealt almost exclusively with Gullah (see Map 2a) but linguists like Stewart (1968) and Dillard (1972) are now suggesting that it is more profitable and more realistic to look at NNE not as a deviant dialect of British English but as a development of a creole English. In other words, according to the schema proposed in this chapter, NNE might be thought of as a creole which has reached what we may call phase 5; that is, an original phase 4 creole which has been decreolized to such an extent that it merges with the standard in many ways. It can be argued that NNE, because of its greater exposure to standard English, has retained fewer creole features and fewer lexical items of African origin than any other pidgin or creole English of the Atlantic type; but it is a verifiable fact that it possesses characteristics usually associated with Atlantic pidgins and creoles.

In NNE there is frequently no overt copula (see Table 27). Often, too, intonation alone distinguishes a question from a

Table 27

Standard	NNE	Cameroon pidgin
I am well	*a well*	*a wel*
you are strong	*you strong, man*	*yu trɔng, bo*

Table 28

Standard	NNE	Krio
do/did you hear?	*you hear?*	*yu yɛri?*
do/did you understand?	*you dig?*	*yu sabi?*

Table 29

Standard	NNE	Jamaican creole
where is he?	*where he is?*	*we i de?*
what does he do?	*what he do?*	*wa im du?*

Table 30

Standard	NNE	Cameroon pidgin
that man is glad	*dat man he glad*	*dat man i glad*
this woman is tired	*dis woman she tired*	*dis woman i taia*

statement (Table 28). Where a question word is used, there is often no inversion (Table 29). In NNE the subject is frequently recapitulated (Table 30).

As in most of the Atlantic pidgins and creoles *bad* can be used as an intensive in NNE: *You like it? Bad!* 'Do you like it? Very much!' Furthermore, one can make a strong case for suggesting that the important feature in the verb phrase is the duration of the action rather than the time of its occurrence. This feature of NNE would connect it not only with other Atlantic pidgins and creoles but with many West African languages as well. In NNE *a readin* can mean, depending on context, 'I am/was/will be reading (at a particular point in time)' and *a be readin* refers to an activity that occurs over a period of time and is not limited to a particular situation. Although one cannot find many examples of African items like *nyam* (found in a large number of Bantu languages with the meaning of 'meat' and/or 'animal') in NNE's vocabulary one does find in American English, and consequently in world English, words which have passed into the language through NNE and which have close parallels in West African languages. As one might expect many of these words are connected with music. Dalby (1970b) has found close West African analogues for 'jazz, jitterbug, jam-(session), jive, boogie-woogie, banjo and hep-cat' to list a few of the eighty Americanisms for which he suggests a West African origin (p. 47). Indeed, if Dalby is right, NNE may have given America and hence the world 'okay', because very similar forms meaning 'yes, yes indeed' occur in a variety of West African languages including Mandingo and Wolof, and a form 'oh ki' is recorded from Jamaica before 'okay' is recorded from the USA.

The selection of similarities between NNE and the Atlantic pidgins and creoles is meant, at most, to be suggestive. It is very probable that a creole English or extended pidgin had taken root on the West African coast as early as the seventeenth century and that some of the slaves shipped to the various parts of the Americas spoke it before they arrived there. Much more research will have to be done before this suggestion can be proved. But that some form of English was widely used on the West African coast in the eighteenth century is evidenced by Labarthe, who complained that British traders had an enormous advantage over other nationalities because they did not need interpreters, since English was spoken along the entire Guinea coast (1803, p. 70). The fact that similarities can be shown to exist between NNE and pidgin and creole Englishes on both sides of the Atlantic may mean that we should think in terms of a New World continuum of English creoles, one that stretched from Surinam and Guyana in the south, through the West Indies, to the USA, a continuum of creoles that are now at different stages of decreolization, the Surinam varieties being the least and the US varieties being the most decreolized. If one agrees, and I personally feel that the evidence favours it, that NNE is probably a creole in an advanced stage of decreolization, then a phase 5 must be postulated to cover it. It is an intriguing possibility that phase 6 may be, in effect, complete coalescence with the standard language.

If educationists see NNE as part of a creole continuum rather than as a debased form of standard English, then two causes may well be served: the teaching of internationally acceptable English should be facilitated since teachers and pupils will be encouraged to realize that they are dealing with a *different* and not a *deficient* variety of English, one which has its own grammatical patterns and systematicity; and speakers of NNE may learn to take pride in one of the first forms of English heard in the Americas. Such recognition might also lead to an examination of the contribution made to American and world English by NNE. After all, Africans speaking a form of creole English were among the first settlers in America. It would be hard to believe that they did not contribute to the development of American English.

From pidgin to creole and thence perhaps to standard English. As yet, the complete circle has not been drawn. In order that a clear progression might be shown phases have been marked as being discrete when they may well have co-occurred. It is likely that phase 2 overlapped phase 1 and that, in the same area, one may have found phases 1, 2 and 3 co-existent at approximately the same period. This chapter is more interested in helping account for processes of expansion in pidgins than in insisting on a specific time scheme. It tries to make clear that there is no stage where one can say: 'Pidgins stop here and creoles begin.' Sharp edges and watertight compartments are rarely found in human languages.

Chapter five

The scope of pidgins and creoles

aiɔn no fit hɔt if yu no putam fɔ faia (iron no fit hot if you no put it for fire). An iron cannot get hot if you don't put it in the fire, i.e. Nothing can succeed if it is not tried.

Our attention in this chapter will focus on creoles and extended pidgins rather than on the extreme phases hypothesized earlier. A restricted pidgin can only either expand or die and the potential of international languages is too well known to need documenting. From the evidence examined it is clear that pidgins and creoles are capable, or can easily become capable, of expressing the needs, opinions and desires of their speakers. In the case of English-based varieties, since the entire lexicon of English is potential pidgin/creole material, no subject is automatically excluded as being beyond their lexical scope. During the Second World War Neo-Melanesian was used for government propaganda, a service to which Nigerian pidgin was also put during the Civil War; politicians have found that Krio is a decided asset in Sierra Leone speech-making; Cameroon pidgin has been used in a broadcast advising listeners of the dangers of leprosy; and all the English varieties have been found adequate for the teaching of a doctrine involving such concepts as 'grace', 'redemption', 'transubstantiation' and 'three divine persons in one God'. As spoken media their potential is at least as great as any other language, greater than some in that they facilitate inter-communication over wide areas; but in an increasingly literate world it is arguable that if they are to survive they must also show their value as written media.

In the past, pidgins and creoles have been almost exclusively spoken languages, but this fact has not prevented their sustaining a vital literature, albeit an oral one. Atlantic pidgins and creoles have, for centuries, been the vehicles for proverbs and workchants, songs and folktales. The African love of storytelling found expression in whatever language adults were obliged to use to children. Like all traditional raconteurs, African storytellers introduced modifications to suit the area and the listeners, but the same basic stories have been recorded thousands of miles apart and across language barriers. The theme of two large animals being manipulated into having a tug-o'-war by the local trickster has turned up in the French-based creoles of Louisiana and Mauritius and in Cameroon pidgin English; many of Harris's Brer Rabbit stories have equivalents in hundreds of West African townships; and the Georgian 'Tar Baby Story' told by Jones (1888, pp. 7–11) is found both in the Krio of Freetown and in Seychellois creole. Such an oral literature, one that has survived changes of culture and language, suggests that these pidgins and creoles are also capable of sustaining a written literature. The further fact that they have successfully transmitted folk wisdom indicates that they might also be employed in formal education. To gauge their value and potential in these spheres it is important to examine how they have already been used and to ask how and whether this usage may be continued, expanded or discarded.

Use in literature

(a) *Literature in pidgins and creoles*   This can conveniently be subdivided into ecclesiastical and non-ecclesiastical works. Writings pertaining to Christianity have been found wherever an English-based pidgin or creole has been widely used. It is hard to say when pidgins and creoles were first employed by missionaries, but it is probable that oral translations of prayers go back at least as far as the eighteenth century. One of the earliest written translations seems to have been the one described by William Hodgson at a meeting of the Ethnological Society of New York on 13 October 1857. He presented to the Society a manuscript in Arabic characters which he described as 'the only attempt ever made by a native African Mohammedan to use the letters of the Koran, the book of his first religious instruction, in transcribing the Gospel, the book of his second instruction and conversion, and in the *adopted dialect* of his land of captivity' (italics mine). The translator, whose name was London, and who was described as a 'Mandingo slave', also wrote a book of hymns which has not survived. Indeed, all that appears to have survived of the gospel is the first verse of St John which Hodgson transliterated as the *Fas chapta ob jon. Inde beginnen wase wad*; *ande wad waswid Gad, ande wad was Gad.* And this merely gives an indication of the pronunciation of the 'adopted dialect', shedding no light on the grammatical patterning of the creole.

From the turn of the twentieth century numerous biblical texts appear. When scholars and missionaries were faced with the task of transcribing pidgins and creoles they had to choose between representing them in a form which approximated to English spelling conventions or in a form which was a more accurate reflection of the language's sound system. The former can be illustrated by Plissoneau's 1926 catechism in Cameroon pidgin: *O good Jesus, I like you, I want you. Come quick for clean my skin and my soul. Come quick for take my heart, and make that I no fit left you again, till the time when you go receive me for heaven. Amen* (p. 109). This type of transcription is interpretable only to those who are proficient in English spelling conventions, but what one should not forget is that such texts were intended to be read *to* and not *by* pidgin speakers.

To choose the second alternative, as was done for Neo-Melanesian by German missionaries before the First World War, meant an orthography like the following: *Dispela em i gutnius bilong Jisas Kraist, Pikinini bilong God. Dispela gutnius em i kamap pastaim olsem profet Aisaia i raitim: 'Harim, mi salim man bilong bringim tok bilong mi, na em i go paslain long yu'* (Gutnius Mak i Raitim, Sapta 1, 1–2, *Nupela Testamen*, 1969, p. 120). Such an orthography has the advantage of being consistent and not dependent on the spelling conventions of any one language but it has a potential disadvantage as well. Neo-Melanesian speakers who are taught this orthography have to learn a different one if they acquire standard English, and there is thus a danger of interference from two conflicting spelling systems.

A third transcription possibility, that of using a phonetically based script, was not used for missionary work. Hall used such a representation in his 1943 work on Neo-Melanesian: *maen i-drimɪm meri, bɪhajn fajnɪm kapul. maen i-lukɪm meri, no mor wašɪm haen, naw i-no kaen lukɪm kapul.* 'If a man dreams about a woman, then he will find a tree kangaroo. But if a man sees a woman (i.e. in his dream) and does not wash his hands, he cannot see the tree kangaroo' (p. 48). It is clear that although this orthography is interpretable by scholars it would not be of much value without phonetic training.

Early missionary attempts often did pidgins and creoles an unwitting injustice by seeming to represent them as unsuccessful efforts at English. To have a text liberally sprinkled with items like *han'*, *'e*, *masta* implied that the form of English was substandard and overlooked the fact that, even in educated speech, 'hand' and 'he' are frequently realized as above and that, in many varieties of standard English, post-vocalic 'r' does not occur. Such a modification of the standard English orthography links these texts with novelists' conventions for representing dialectal and uneducated speech; but although such conventions made for relatively easy reading by English speakers, they contributed to the notion that pidgins and creoles, like dialects, were debased, substandard forms of English.

Recent biblical translations have avoided such unintentional prejudgments and have attempted to use spelling systems based on a phonological analysis of the specific pidgin or creole. In theory, this change is an improvement but the newly established orthographies are, like the Melanesian variety, a potential source of interference. Scholars may be adept at switching from one orthographic system to another, but the practice is not so easy for untrained readers.

As well as missionary writings there is a large body of non-ecclesiastical writing in pidgins and creoles. The best known are from the USA and these were aimed at a non-pidgin-speaking audience which was frequently encouraged to see such language varieties as 'quaint'. The 'Uncle Remus' tales of Harris were immediately popular and led to the publishing of similar works, like Jones, *Negro Myths from the South Georgia Coast* (1888), Milne-Horne, *Mamma's Black Nurse Stories* (1890) and Smith, *Annancy Stories* (1899). Many of the writers who produced such literature had a profound appreciation of the culture of the ex-slaves, and their writings did much to reveal this culture to the white world. Their attitude to the language, however, was often one of condescension. In his preface (1888, p. vi) Jones refers to the area where he collected the tales:

> The swamp region of Georgia and the Carolinas, where the lingo of the rice-field and the sea-island negroes is *sui generis*, and where myths and fanciful stories, often repeated before the war, and now seldom heard save during the gayer moods of the old plantation darkies, materially differ from those narrated by the sable dwellers of the interior.

Whatever Jones's attitude to the people from whom he collected the 'myths', he had a considerable knowledge of their creole and his orthography gives a reasonably accurate indication of Gullah pronunciation even today: *Buh Wolf and Buh Rabbit bin a cote de same Gal. De Gal bin rich and berry pooty. Dem tuk tun fuh wisit um. Buh Rabbit, him gone der mornin, and Buh Wolf, him gone der ebenin. De Gal harde fuh mek up eh mine. Eh sorter courage bofe er um* (p. 27).

Although the best known samples of literature in pidgins and creoles come from the New World, examples can also be cited from China and West Africa. In these areas it is more common to get pidgin and creole passages included as illustrative material rather than to have entire works in these media, though the latter do exist. Charles Leland's *Pidgin English Sing-Song* of 1876 was written in what he called the 'China-English Dialect' (title page). He believed that China coast pidgin was in fact 'English words . . . set forth according to the principles of Chinese grammar. It is . . . word for word translation, with very little attempt at inflection or conjugation, as such forms of grammar, as we understand them, do not exist in Chinese' (p. 1). One wonders how the Chinese would react to such a description of this passage: *One-tim one Jew-man lib Californee-side makee one big piecee bobbely* (trouble, noise) *longside one Chinaman. He callo Chinaman plenty bad name; he callo la-li-loong,* (thief) *all-same tiefman: he too muchee saucy, galaw* (approximately, my word!) (p. 98).

From West Africa came *Cunnie Rabbit, Mister Spider and the Other Beef* (1903), a book of tales collected in the latter half of the nineteenth century and partly transcribed in an approximation to Krio: '*All dem beef* [animals] *en Cunnie Rabbit bin meet up to one place. Now dey pull* [pulled out] *all dem horn, en put um 'pon de groun'. Any beef pull he yown . . . One grain pusson no lef' way get horn, en dey say:* "*De pusson wey blow all dis yeah horn one one* [one by one] *widout he no lef fo' blow, dis one we go take fo' king*" ' (p. 129).

From West Africa also comes a work which seems to be unique in pidgin/creole writings. It is the diary of Antera Duke, an Efik chief, and it contains entries for 1785–8 in an approximation to the pidginized English spoken in Calabar at the time: *1:10:1787 . . . I have see two King aqua women slave com from my yard Break one my god Bason he say will be slave so I Did send word to King aqua to Let us know and after 2 clock wee all 4 Callabar new and old Egbo go to meet to King Ambo plaver house about willy Curcock Egbo palaver* (Forde, 1956, pp. 110–11). 'I saw two of King Aqua's women slaves coming from my yard. They broke one of my god basins and said they would be my slaves. So I sent word to King Aqua to let him know and after two o'clock we all four new and old Calabar Ekpe went to meet at King Ambo's palaver house about Willy Curcock's Ekpe palaver' (p. 60).

From the beginning of the twentieth century pidgins and creoles have become increasingly common in literature, though only rarely has it been the medium of a whole work. The type of English used by Tutuola in such works as *The Palm Wine Drinkard* was not Nigerian pidgin but rather his Yoruba-influenced approximation to English, and similar verdicts could be passed on many of the Onitsha Market novelettes, popular paperbacks published in Onitsha and written mainly by Nigerians, many of whom had only a limited command of English. Sam Selvon, it is true, has written much in what he describes as 'the Trinidadian dialect' but, while this variety evinces many features of West Indian creoles, it is approaching the standard end of the spectrum.

While such literature, both ecclesiastical and non-ecclesiastical, was being written, scholars were producing dictionaries, grammars and descriptions of a number of pidgins and creoles. Many collected and preserved textual samples, especially in the twentieth century, and from the 1940s men like Reinecke and Hall have done a great deal to eliminate prejudice and ignorance; but the scholarly voices tended to whisper in the wilderness and only recently have their aggregated whispers begun to be heard.

(*b*) *Pidgins and creoles in literature*   Apart from the full texts in pidgins and creoles and the scholarly treatises on certain varieties, references to and snippets of pidgin and creole have appeared occasionally in English literature from the early eighteenth century. Daniel Defoe introduced considerable amounts in *Colonel Jacque* (1722): *Master, me speakee de true, they never give Mercièè, they always Whippee, Lashee, Knockee down, all Cruel: Negroe be muchee better Man do muchee better Work, but they tell us no Mercièè* (Defoe, p. 137). It is unlikely that Defoe's Virginian 'pidgin' is based on first- or even second-hand information and this may partly explain why his 'pidgin' so closely resembles the variety reported from the China coast, especially with regard to the '-ee' ending which Defoe singles out as being a chief characteristic of pidgin English: 'all those Natives, as also those of Africa, when they learn English, they always add two E's at the end of the Words where we use one, and make the accent upon them, as *makèè*, *takèè* and the like' (*Farther Adventures of Robinson Crusoe*, 1719, p. 76). One can see these resemblances by referring to Leland's version of Little Jack Horner in China coast pidgin (1876, p. 75):

> *Littee Jack Horner*
> *Makee sit inside corner,*
> *Chow-chow he Clismas pie;*
> *He put inside t'um,*

Hab catchee one plum,
'Hai yah! what one good chilo my!'

Such resemblances might lead one to suspect that literary insertions of pidgins and creoles were, in the past, based less on actual observation than on a form of literary convention which, when taken to extremes, could produce the situation where, according to the popular joke, an Englishman hoping to make a distinguished Chinese diplomat and fellow guest at a dinner party feel more at ease enquired: 'Likee soupee?' Later, the diplomat was invited to make a speech which he did in perfect English and, on sitting down, turned to the Englishman and asked: 'Likee speechee?'

If Defoe's representation of New World pidgin English were based on accurate information one would expect it to have more in common with other Atlantic pidgins and creoles. That quite considerable homogeneity existed throughout the Americas is supported by Hall's quotation of a warrant issued to an American Indian in the seventeenth century: *You, you big constable, quick you catch um Jeremiah Offscow, strong you hold um, safe you bring um afore me, Waban, Justice Peace* (1966, p. 8). This sample resembles other Atlantic varieties in the use of repetition for emphasis, the lack of a copula in an equative sentence (*you big constable*), the use of a third person accusative marker *um*, the neutralization of the distinction between adjectives and adverbs and a reduction of prepositions. Defoe's use of pidgin was almost certainly a stylistic device used to lend verisimilitude to his supposedly real-life adventures as well as to supply a touch of the exotic. He does not appear to have intended it to be humorous though political cartoonists were quick to seize on this aspect of pidgin English. Cruikshank (1819), for example, satirizes the West Indian 'Master' with the bible in one hand and a whip in the other when he has his negro caricature say: *One thing at a time Massa if you please,—if you floggee—floggee—if you preachee preachee —but no preachee and floggee too* (*Pigmy Revels or All Alive at Lilliput*, Plate 2). Still others adopted a condescending attitude towards it, suggesting that nothing other than this form of English could be expected from a black man. Anthony Trollope typified this attitude when, referring to the West Indies, he claimed: 'But the eye soon becomes accustomed to the black skin and the thick lip, and the ear to the broken patois which is the nearest approach to English which the ordinary negro ever makes'(1859,p. 55). Lady Nugent, a less prejudiced observer, gave the lie to this type of suggestion when she drew attention to the fact that 'the creole language is not confined to the negroes' (Diary entry, 24 April 1802, p. 98).

In the areas of the world where pidgin and creole Englishes developed it was, until the twentieth century, rare to find other than the whites experimenting with such forms in literature. With the spread of education and the growth of self-assurance, however, many writers realized that to deny their mother tongues or the language in which they most readily communicated with outsiders was to impair their creativity. Throughout the anglophone areas of West Africa and the West Indies novelists, poets and dramatists realized the imaginative and humorous potential of pidgins and creoles. The lack of a uniform orthography and of standardized norms were considerable handicaps, but the advantages of employing such a medium outweighed the drawbacks. Early efforts were often tentative and exploratory, but in writers like Achebe there is a clear development in his use of Nigerian pidgin. In *No Longer at Ease* (1960) he uses it half apologetically for humorous purposes: 'Joseph always put on an impressive manner when speaking on the telephone. He never spoke Ibo or pidgin English at such moments. When he hung up he told his colleagues: "*That na my brother, just return from overseas. BA (Honours) Classics.*" He always preferred the fiction of Classics to the truth of English. It sounded more impressive' (p. 77). From such a tentative use Achebe comes to a full realization of its potential in *Girls at War* (1972). In this volume of stories pidgin facilitates character drawing and also functions as a choric medium for the writer's grim humour (1972, pp. 94–5):

Maria was the first to raise the alarm, then he followed and all their children.

'Police-o! Thieves-o! Neighbours-o! Police-o! We are lost!
We are dead! Neighbours, are you asleep? Wake up!
Police-o!'
This went on for a long time and then stopped suddenly.
Perhaps they had scared their thief away. There was total
silence. But only for a short while.
'*You done finish?*' asked the voice outside. '*Make we help you
small. Oya, everybody!*'
'*Police-o! Tief-man-o! Neighbours-o! we done loss-o!
Police-o! . . .*'
. . . The silence that followed the thieves' alarm vibrated
horribly. Jonathan all but begged their leader to speak again
and be done with it.
'*My frien,*' said he at long last, '*we don try our best for call dem
but I tink say dem all done sleep-o . . . So wetin we go do now?
Somtaim you wan call soja? Or you wan make we call dem for
you? Soja better pass police. No be so?*'

It was the humorous potential of pidgins and creoles which
was first explored, but writers who used the languages with
sensitivity soon realized that they need not be restricted to
humour, that pidgins and creoles could serve a tragic function
too. This is clearly shown in Trefossa's Surinam creole poem
which has been translated by Voorhoeve and in which the
speaker, an educated, widely travelled creole user, sees the
value of his own early experiences but is, as it were, lost
between two cultures (Hymes, 1971, pp. 324–6):

mi go—m'e kon	I've gone—I come
te dreeten winti sa trotji	if the dry season wind starts
na Mawnidan:	singing in Mahogany Street:
—krioro fa?	—Creole, how?
m'sa pitji:	I'll answer:
—dja mi de,	—here am I,
—banji fu ba-m'ma seti keba:	—granny's bench has been set ready
—ertintin . . . ertintin . . .	—once upon a time . . . once upon a time . . .
te dreeten winti sa trotji	if the dry season wind starts singing

na kankantri:	in the cotton-tree:
—krioro fa?	—Creole, how?
m'sa pitji:	I'll answer:
—dja mi de,	—here am I,
—Eifeltoren hee passa,	—Eifel Tower is much higher,
—m'a n'a jorka, a n'a	—but has no spirits, has no
iorka . . .	spirits . . .
te dreeten winti sa trotji	if the dry season wind starts singing
na Moi-bon fu Bose:	in Big Tree of Bose:
—krioro fa?	—Creole, how?
m'sa pitji:	I'll answer:
—dja mi de,	—here am I,
—s'sa Mina, ptata bun,	—Sister Mary, potatoes are all right,
—ma bojo fu ju tjir-tjiri . . .	—but your cake is just the best . . .
mi go—m'e kon,	I've gone—I come,
sootwatra bradi.	the sea is wide.
tak wan mofo,	say the words,
ala mi mati,	you all my friends,
tak wan mofo.	say the words.
m'go,	I've gone,
m'e kon . . .	I come . . .

And yet it would be wrong to suggest that pidgins and creoles have been restricted to extremes of humour or pathos. They have shown themselves to be as flexible and versatile as their users have wanted them to be. West Indian and West African literary work has received much academic attention, but very little has been written about literature in Neo-Melanesian, though as early as 1939 it was found adequate for the poetic expression of homesickness (Hogbin, 1939, p. vii):

Ples bilong mi i namerwan,	Place belong me (i = verbal marker) number one,
Mi laikim im tasol.	Me like him that's all.
Mi tink long papa, mama tu,	Me think along father, mother too,
Mi krai long haus blong ol.	Me cry along house belong all.

Mi wok long ples i longwe tru,	Me work along place long way true,
Mi stap no gud tasol.	Me stop no good that's all.
Ples bilong mi i namberwan,	Place belong me number one,
Mi laikim im tasol.	Me like him that's all.
Ol wantok, brader, susa tu,	All one talk [i.e. people who speak the same language] brothers, sisters too,
Long taim i wetim mi.	Long time wait for me.
Ol salim planti tok i kam,	All send plenty talk come,
Ol tink mi lus long si.	All think me lost along sea.
Nau mi kirap, mi go long ples,	Now me get up, me go along place,
Mi no kin lusim mor.	Me no can lose him more.
Ples bilong mi i namberwan,	Place belong me number one,
Mi laikim im tasol.	Me like him that's all.

Since Neo-Melanesian is very likely to become accepted as an official language of Papua New Guinea when it becomes independent, and since it is already used in instruction manuals, advertisements, newspapers and public notices, its full exploitation as a literary medium cannot be far distant. Nor is Neo-Melanesian the only pidgin to be so extensively used. Similar uses for all the pidgin and creole Englishes referred to could be cited. The fact that pidgins and creoles have established such a foothold in the written medium suggests that they might well be employed in education.

Use in education

It can no longer be seriously suggested that pidgins and creoles are incapable of being used as media of instruction. As has been shown, the tenets of Christianity and the folk wisdom of African peoples and peoples of African descent have frequently been taught in this way. The debatable point is not whether they *could* be used but whether they *should* be. And a decision on this point could have important implications not only in countries where a pidgin or creole is a vital lingua franca but also in countries like Britain which have large West Indian populations. If an evaluation of the evidence suggests that pidgins and creoles ought to be employed in the classroom or at least properly understood by the teacher then such a decision could have a direct bearing on the teaching of English in immigrant communities.

(a) *The oral use of a pidgin or creole in the classroom*   No-one will argue with the proposition that education depends on communication, a two-way communication between pupil and teacher; and the most obvious medium for such communication is language. But in a pidgin or creole situation which language should be used? In an area like Surinam where English is not the country's official language and where three well-defined and widely used creoles exist it seems reasonable that creole speakers be taught through the medium of their own language, especially in rural areas where Dutch is an officially recognized but totally unknown language. (Such a programme is already in existence in Surinam where Djuka is being used in a literacy campaign.) In areas where standard English continues to be an official or prestige language the answer is less obvious. In such areas, as we have seen in chapter 4, there is usually no clear dividing line between the pidgin or creole and the standard, and most individuals can use several varieties of the spectrum. To insist that, in these areas, standard English should always be the medium of both teacher and pupil is shortsighted. In the first place few of the pupils starting school will have control of a variety at the standard end of the spectrum. Furthermore, while the teachers are assumed to have such a mastery, they can rarely sustain a teaching programme entirely in standard English since in these countries, as elsewhere, the tendency is to put the least qualified staff in charge of beginners. But even if they could sustain such a programme, to do so might well mean talking above the linguistic competence of their pupils; and this could result in either alienation or a complete break-down in communications.

In pidgin- and creole-speaking areas it seems to me reasonable to admit the use of some form of the lingua franca in oral education, especially in the first year of primary education, and also in the initial stages of adult literacy campaigns. This is not so much a defeatist attitude as an attempt to be realistic in the face of the needs, aspirations and levels of competence of both pupil and teacher. To instil in teachers while they are in training colleges the knowledge that the occasional use of the pidgin or creole might well be sound pedagogical practice— for example in supplying the local equivalent of an unknown English word or phrase—might have the effect of reducing unnecessary classroom tension. A teacher who does not have to worry unduly about his own linguistic performance might be more sensitive to the type of language most useful in encouraging individual pupils to participate in classroom work. This does not mean that a teacher can disregard language standards. Nor does it mean he can run the risk of appearing condescending. It does, however, take cognizance of the fact that in the majority of classroom situations in pidgin- and creole-speaking areas one has a microcosm of a post-creole continuum with the teacher's performance approaching the standard end. As far as oral behaviour is concerned the aim should be to facilitate the pupil's manipulation of a wider range of varieties, ultimately resulting in his ability to control standard English.

(b) *The use of a pidgin or creole as a written medium in the classroom* A limited use of pidgins and creoles in oral instruction seems justified, on pedagogic grounds, in early stages of education. Socially too it seems acceptable since it is likely that future linguistic contact for the majority of pupils in any area is regional rather than international. At first sight the use of pidgins and creoles in the teaching of reading and writing might also seem to be reasonable. This is not, however, the case. It has already been noted that the orthographic problems posed by pidgins and creoles are considerable. There is little doubt that individual orthographies could be worked out for each pidgin and creole, but which part of the spectrum should be isolated as the norm? And whose pronunciation should be selected as the model?

It could be argued that just as the oral use of the local pidgin or creole might initially be of help in primary schools, so too might texts in it facilitate the acquisition of the reading and writing skills in the pidgin or creole, skills which might then be transferred to reading and writing in standard English. This is possibly true. Pidgin and creole texts might indeed contribute to this acquisition, but at what cost? Even waiving financial considerations, the psychological cost would veto such a project. If educationists decide to use such texts they face serious problems. If they use the standard English orthography they save money on printing but make the pidgin or creole appear at best dialectal, at worst inferior. And if they use a tailor-made orthography they teach a set of spelling conventions which will inevitably clash with those of standard English. At this point one can see where the skills associated with reading and writing differ from those associated with speech. While pidgin and creole speakers may spend most of their lives in a pidgin- or creole-speaking area, the majority of what they read and write will, of necessity, be in standard English, whether it be an examination paper, a novel, an official notice or a letter of application for employment. Admittedly, each area must be considered separately. One might well wish to exclude Surinam, for example, and perhaps also Papua New Guinea from the above generalizations, largely because in both these areas a form of the creole and the pidgin stands a good chance of becoming an officially used and recognized language. In such cases one can foresee a time when the majority of publications for local use will be in these languages; but until such a time and until such a policy is clearly envisaged it seems unproductive to teach reading and writing by means of pidgin or creole texts in a special orthography—unproductive in that by so doing one inculcates habits at a formative stage, habits which may interfere with the later acquisition of the more useful conventions of standard English spelling.

But have I not put forward conflicting possibilities? A partial acceptance of an oral use of pidgins and creoles in the classroom and a rejection of their written use, together with the rejection of a special orthography? I suggest that the conflict is only apparent. To begin with, the spoken language allows for more flexibility than the written. Years of intensive

educational effort to eradicate dialectal speech habits in
Northern Ireland have failed because there is no compelling
reason to acquire the British standard. Indeed, to some mem-
bers of this community the home dialect, and in particular the
home accent, is seen as a valued badge of identity. But such
clinging to speech habits has not hindered the acquisition of
the grammatical and spelling conventions of written English.
In addition, the international English orthography is only
very tenuously connected with pronunciation. The fact that
'three' may be pronounced 'free' by a Cockney child and
'tree' by a Jamaican need not, necessarily, affect their written
performance. Furthermore, there is no serious problem of com-
prehension if the Jamaican or the Irish child continues to
pronounce /θ/ as /t/. No moral canons have been broken.
One might even regard it as an overgeneralization of the rule
that allows educated Southern British speakers to pronounce
'Anthony' as if it were 'Antony'.

To be liberal in educational policies is, in theory, excellent
as long as the liberality does not penalize the recipients. In
our world, for people to be literate in any meaningful sense is
to be able to read and write the standard languages. When such
a level of literacy has been reached one can then adapt the
standard English orthography to suit the special literary needs
of a pidgin or a creole. It is even arguable that because the
standard English orthography reflects no specific pronunciation
with any precision it is as capable of representing a whole
spectrum of pidgin/creole pronunciations as it now represents
various British, American, Australian and Indian pronunciations. I have no doubt that pidgins and creoles will continue
to be used in literature, will continue to be popular in advertisements and in the press, but it is significant that all those who
have used these languages efficiently, in the written medium,
have also been masters of the standard form.

It is not that pidgins and creoles are incapable of being
used as media of instruction; rather that, with a few exceptions,
to do so is impractical and educationally disadvantageous.
Initial ease of acquisition may exact an unacceptably high
price—the limiting of literacy for many to the pidgin or the

creole. This price is doubly unacceptable when one realizes that a similar ease of acquisition could be achieved by using culturally relevant material in the standard language. Educationists and theorists may argue for a widespread use of pidgin and creole Englishes in the classroom, but such a policy is rarely in keeping with the desires of the parents or with the mature needs of the pupils. Education is meant to open doors, not to barricade them from within.

Chapter six

Conclusion

> *dat bɛlɛ we rɛbrɛn kɔmɔt, na di tifman kɔmɔt*   (that belly which
> reverend come out, be the thiefman come out). The womb from
> which the clergyman came also gave birth to the robber, i.e.
> Very different exteriors can hide similar origins.

In the past, pidgins and creoles with lexical affinities to European languages were often misunderstood and disparaged.
Because they were associated with populations which had been
enslaved or with peoples whose cultures differed radically
from those of western Europe, they were regarded as inferior
languages, the use of which was often seen as a reflection of
mental inferiority. Nor are such feelings entirely dead, though
their expression is, today, more muted. 1971 could still produce
a remark like: 'I feel that modern linguists have been danger-
ously sentimental about creole languages, which, with only a
few notable exceptions, constitute in most communities a distinct handicap to the social mobility of the individual and *may*
also constitute a handicap to the creole speaker's personal
intellectual development' (Whinnom, p. 110). In multilingual
communities it is clear that geographical mobility is increased
rather than sacrificed by the acquisition of a pidgin or a creole,
though if a person speaks only a creole he may certainly be
hampered if he wishes to be internationally mobile. There
seems much less justification, however, for the suggestion that
a creole may be detrimental to a creole speaker's 'intellectual
development', for how can such an abstraction be measured?
And even if it could be measured, from whose point of view
would it be considered a handicap? It is perhaps plausible that
if a group were limited to the use of a restricted pidgin their
communicative powers might be impaired; but no group of
people has ever, apparently, allowed itself to be so hampered.
The Africans taken to the Americas expanded and developed

their pidgins, utilizing many sources until their creoles became capable of expressing all their linguistic needs. That certain Europeans found the languages restricting is hardly surprising if they did not learn them properly. An English schoolboy may find it inhibiting to express his needs in French but the 'fault' lies not in the language but in the boy's ability to manipulate it. This fact was realized as early as 1869 when Thomas remarked that if a person wished to use the French-based Trinidadian creole, he 'must, for the while, forget his French, and believe (for it is a fact) that he is using a dialect fully capable of expressing all ordinary thoughts, provided the speaker is master of, and understands how to manage, its resources' (1869, p. 105).

The previous chapters show that pidgins and creoles are not intrinsically different from other languages. No single feature exhibited by pidgins and creoles is unique to these languages, though the co-occurrence of features such as lack of inflection, rigidity of word order, loss or reduction of distinctions relating to number, gender and agreement, may be indicative of prior pidginization. But, as has been suggested, pidginization or language simplification and adjustment is common to all situations where languages have come into contact. Furthermore, it is clear that widely used pidgins and creoles are capable of serving all the needs of the community, including, should it prove necessary or useful, their educational and literary needs. Such a possibility ceases to be merely theoretical when one considers the role, position and achievements of Afrikaans. The sociological documentation provided by Valkhoff in 1966 and 1972 indicates that Dutch was being pidginized in the Cape Province by non-Dutch speakers in the latter half of the seventeenth century and creolized in racially mixed domestic households. Valkhoff quotes the following extract from van Rheede's 1685 report (1972, pp. 40-1):

> There is a custom here among all our people that when these natives [i.e. the Hottentots] learn the Dutch language and speak it, in their manner very badly and hardly intelligibly, our people imitate them in this so that, as the children of our Dutchmen

also fall into the habit, a broken language is founded which it will be impossible to overcome later on.

I have introduced Afrikaans to illustrate how a language which has been pidginized may develop structures which differ considerably from the lexical source language, in this case Dutch (see Table 31). And yet Afrikaans has become a language not only of trade but capable of handling all aspects of life in a technologically advanced twentieth-century society. But it also poses a question. If we had not known the history of Afrikaans and if Dutch no longer existed would one be able to postulate that Dutch had been pidginized and creolized in a multilingual society? One might list features of Afrikaans which suggest

Table 31

Dutch	Afrikaans	English
Het kan me niet schelen	*Ek gie nie om nie*	I don't mind
Hij heeft gelijk	*Hy is reg*	He is right
Maak haast	*Maak gou-gou*	Hurry up

prior pidginization, such as structural simplicity when compared with Germanic languages, serial verb structures like 'sit die kinders *sit speel*', 'the children are sitting and playing', reduplication, features which some linguists consider to be creole universals. But it seems important to point out that a purely synchronic analysis of Afrikaans might well prove inconclusive and that only a comparison with past and present forms of Dutch can support the Valkhoffian theory that South African Dutch was creolized in the seventeenth century.

Nor is this situation limited to Afrikaans or to recognized world creoles. Modern English, when compared with the forms of the language which existed in England prior to the Norman Conquest, also reveals many features consistent with pidginization, as indeed does French when compared with Classical Latin. In all of these examples a recurrent concept has been 'comparison', a fact which allows one to postulate that many languages which have not been classified as creoles and whose histories are not known may also have undergone processes of simplification. This suggests an interesting corollary, namely that the creole universals which are being established from a close analysis of world pidgins and creoles may prove insightful in analysing languages whose histories and origins have not been overtly documented. If this view is correct, and the processes of simplification and accommodation are similar wherever people, not rigidly bound by conventions of 'standard languages', come into contact, then the linguistic features which are common to pidgins and creoles may prove as valuable a parameter in the study of the history of languages as the study of sound changes was in the past. The existence of pidgins and creoles ought also to instil in students of language a caution with regard to the notion that language change is gradual, continuous and regular. The history of pidgin and creole languages from the fifteenth century clearly shows that social upheavals resulting from contact situations can create conditions in which languages can change very markedly in one or two generations. Nor is there any reason to believe that this was not always the case where peoples and languages were in contact, though the changes brought about in any language would be related to the degrees of difference in the languages involved in the contact.

Historical and contemporary data strongly suggest that when an Indo-European language is adopted under conditions of stress by a speaker of a mutually unintelligible language, then inflection tends to be reduced or lost and the determination of categories like subject, predicate, object, becomes largely dependent on word order. In Classical Latin different word order could indicate different emphases but 'Paul loves Mary' would be understood from:

Mariam amat Paulus
Amat Mariam Paulus
Paulus Mariam amat
Paulus amat Mariam

The same permutations are not possible in French where the same idea would normally be expressed by 'Paul aime Marie'.

Rigidity of word order in this sentence compensates for loss of inflection. Modern English has a more rigid word order than Anglo-Saxon and the word order in Neo-Melanesian is more rigid than either. Such knowledge raises the possibility that languages with relatively rigid word order are more likely to have been in close contact with other languages or to have been used as lingua francas. (According to linguistic purists the correct plural of 'lingua franca' is 'lingue franche'. I prefer to anglicize the term.)

Pidgins and creoles have long been the 'poor relations' in the world's language families, relegated to the kitchen or the fields, thought to be devoid of cultural potential, dismissed as hotch-potch languages, undervalued and inadequately understood. It may well be, however, that they are simply modern results of universal principles and that they appear so conspicuous because the languages which furnished their vocabularies still exist and have prestige. Linguists and sociologists have acknowledged their value in permitting communication where it was previously unknown; and their value to scholarship may be much higher than has previously been supposed. They may give insights into language change and development, may help in the discovery and formulation of linguistic universals, and may be a partial key to the problem of why fixed word order is a concomitant of some but not all languages, or at some but not all stages of a language's existence.

This study of pidgins and creoles has tended to put a higher value on them than has usually been the case. It has tried to show that it is shortsighted to dismiss them as 'debased jargons'. Pidgins and creoles are languages which have facilitated and are facilitating communication and freedom of movement in multilingual communities, and which are capable of expressing the ideas and ideals of their users. From the point of view of scholarly research they offer a new dimension in the study of linguistic history and provide data in the search for linguistic universals. Their value to various communities, especially in the past, has been emphasized. Whether the future will put a premium on the continued existence of such languages, whether in the twentieth century any contemporary creoles can become self-sustaining languages, or whether international communication with its dependence on a limited number of standard languages will cause their extinction are questions which one must leave open. But if they become extinct it will not be because of any intrinsic linguistic inadequacies but because they cannot compete against the overwhelming pressures of standard English. Their extinction would be due to the same socio-economic reasons that are causing Irish Gaelic, for example, to die out. In theory one could argue for their cultivation as international lingua francas. Alfred de Saint-Quentin recognized this over a hundred years ago when he claimed (1872, pp. lviii–lix):

> Une analyse sérieuse m'a convaincu d'un fait qui paraîtra paradoxal. C'est que si l'on voulait créer de toutes pièces une langue générale qui permît, après quelques jours d'étude seulement, un échange clair et régulier d'idées simples, on ne saurait adopter des bases plus logiques et plus fécondes que celles de la syntaxe creole.
> (A close analysis has convinced me of what may appear paradoxical. It is that if one wanted to assemble a general language which would, after a few days' study, allow a clear and systematic exchange of simple ideas, one could not choose a more logical or fruitful foundation than that of creole syntax.)

But in practice it is unlikely that the major world languages will be replaced by any other language, however simple, however logical, whether that language is Esperanto or one of the world's pidgins or creoles. These latter have been invaluable in the past and their immediate existence is less in jeopardy than many unwritten languages, but in the long run they may, like other languages, die out if their usefulness comes to an end. In this as in so many other respects, they are like all other languages. The Krio proverb which prefaced this chapter is applicable to languages as well as people, and underlines the importance of remembering that languages may appear different, but external divergence hides the fact that they differ in form, not in fundamentals.

Appendix one

Pidgin and creole languages referred to together with an indication of the area where they are most widely known and used.

Language	*Area*
Antiguan creole English	Antigua
Bamboo English	Mainly in Korea during the American-Korean war. (A similar variety is said to have existed in Japan during the Second World War and to be in existence in Vietnam since the American escalation of the war there.)
Beach-la-Mar	Islands between Asia and Australia. (It is an offshoot of China coast pidgin English and is gradually being replaced by its own offshoot, Neo-Melanesian.)
Cameroon pidgin English	Cameroon
China coast pidgin English	China coast (now becoming extinct).
Chinook Jargon	North West Canada
Djuka	Surinam
Ewondo Populaire	Around the Cameroon capital, Yaoundé.
Gullah	Sea Islands and the strip of coast from Florida to South Carolina.
Haitian creole	Haiti
Honduras creole English	British Honduras
Jamaican creole	Jamaica
Krio	Around Freetown in Sierra Leone, throughout Sierra Leone and in various

Language	*Area*
	West African ports where Krio speakers from Freetown settled.
Malay	A pidginized form of High Malay is a useful lingua franca throughout Malaysia and Indonesia. It is sometimes referred to as 'Bazaar Malay'.
Mbugu	Tanzania
Neo-Melanesian	Around Port Moresby and throughout Papua New Guinea. (A closely related pidgin, also descended from Beach-la-Mar, is spoken in the British Solomon Islands.)
Nigerian pidgin English	Nigeria
Papiamentu	Curaçao
Pitcairnese	Pitcairn Island. (A related creole English, called Norfolkese, is spoken on Norfolk Island by settlers from Pitcairn.)
Police Motu	Mainly in and around Port Moresby in PNG
Sango	Central African Republic
Saramaccan	Surinam
Seychellois	Seychelles
Sranan	Surinam
Swahili	Several pidginized and creolized versions of Swahili exist in East and Central Africa. (Evidence suggests that Swahili itself may be the result of contact between Arabic and Bantu languages.)

Appendix two

Other, less well-known, languages referred to and an indication of the area where they are most widely used.

Bemba	Rhodesian copperbelt
Ewe	Ghana
Ewondo	In and around Yaoundé, in Cameroon.
Hausa	Northern Nigeria and as a lingua franca among West African Muslims.
Igbo	Southern Nigeria
Lamso	South-West Cameroon
Mandingo	Gambia and Senegal and as an auxiliary language in neighbouring areas of West Africa.
Motu	In the neighbourhood of Port Moresby in Papua New Guinea.
Ngbandi	Central African Republic
Twi	Ghana
Wolof	Senegambia
Yoruba	Western Nigeria
Zulu	South-East Africa

Appendix three

Many rural peoples encapsulate traditional wisdom in the form of proverbs. Pidgin- and creole-speaking communities are no exception. The proverbs quoted in this book come from West Africa and in particular from Cameroon and Sierra Leone, though the folk wisdom they express is to be found, in slightly modified form, in many of the Atlantic pidgin/creole-speaking regions and may well reflect original African proverbs and folk-beliefs.

1 trɔki	wan	fait	bɔt	i	sabi	sei	i	han	shɔt
↓	↓	↓	↓	↓	↓	↓	↓	↓	↓
tortoise	want	fight	but	he	know	say	he	hand	short

This proverb comes from Cameroon and comparable forms are found in Nigeria and Sierra Leone. In many pidgins and creoles *han* < 'hand' encompasses the meaning of both 'hand' and 'arm', just as *fut* < 'foot' can mean both 'foot' and 'leg'.

2 bɔn	mi,	a	fiva	yu
↓	↓	↓	↓	↓
born	me,	I	favour	you (favour = resemble)

This proverb also comes from Cameroon and is to be found, in slightly modified form, throughout anglophone West Africa.

3 yu	tink	sei	na	kapenta	klin	mi?
↓	↓	↓	↓	↓	↓	↓
you	think	say	be	carpenter	clean	me

This is a Cameroonian expression which often implies 'I'm not made of wood'. There are three BE-verbs in Cameroon pidgin: *na* used in equative, identifying sentences e.g.
pita na kapenta—Peter is a carpenter
dei used in locative sentences e.g.
pita dei fɔ haus—Peter is in the house

bi which can be used in both the above type sentences. Its use is increasing in Cameroon. *klin* illustrates the extension of meaning which many words have undergone in pidgins and creoles. It can mean 'clean' but also, in this case, 'whittle', 'carve'.

4 dɔg	drim	lɛf	na	im	bɛlɛ
dog	dream	leave	in	he	belly

This Krio proverb illustrates the use of *na* as a locative preposition. Its etymology is not certain but its form and meaning are similar to Portuguese 'na' (see p. 36). In many parts of West Africa the 'belly' is thought to be the seat of the emotions.

5 if	a	no	pas		sliv,	a	pas		pɔkɛt
if	I	no	pass (surpass)		sleeve	I	pass (surpass)		pocket

pas is used in many of the Atlantic pidgins and creoles to mean 'surpass' and it is used in comparative structures:
i big pas mi—(he big pass (surpass) me)—he is bigger than I. This proverb also has wide currency in anglophone West Africa.

6 aiɔn	no	fit	hɔt	if	yu	no	putam	fɔ	faia
iron	no	fit	hot	if	you	no	put + it	for	fire

In Cameroon pidgin the preposition *fɔ* is among the most frequently used lexemes. Its use is one distinguishing mark between Cameroon pidgin and Krio. Krio tends to use *na* where Cameroon pidgin uses *fɔ*.

7 dat	bɛlɛ	we	rɛbrɛn	kɔmɔt,		na	di	tifman		kɔmɔt
that	belly	which	reverend	come + out		be	the	thief + man		come + out

This Krio proverb illustrates the use of *na* as a verb. The exact origin of the essive verb *na* is unknown.

Suggestions for further reading

CASSIDY, F. G. (1961) *Jamaica Talk: Three Hundred Years of the English Language in Jamaica*, London, Macmillan.
This book provides the historical and social backdrop necessary to appreciate the linguistic characteristics of Jamaican creole. It keeps technical terms to a minimum and provides a most comprehensive picture of a creole community.
DUTTON, T. E. (1973) *Conversational New Guinea Pidgin*, Pacific Linguistics, Series D, 12, Canberra. The most up-to-date analysis of Neo-Melanesian, or 'Tok Pisin' as it is referred to locally.
Dutton's comprehensive course has an accompanying set of tapes.
GOODMAN, MORRIS (1964) *A Comparative Study of Creole French Dialects*, The Hague, Mouton.
Some knowledge of French is necessary for a full appreciation of Goodman. This book is particularly useful for the data it provides on French-based creoles, data which can be compared with studies of other European-language-based pidgins and creoles.
HALL, ROBERT A., JR (1966) *Pidgin and Creole Languages*, Ithaca, Cornell University Press.
This simply written, widely researched book is an easy introduction to the concept of pidgins and creoles. It contains many useful illustrations from a wide variety of languages.
HYMES, DELL, ed. (1971) *Pidginization and Creolization of Languages*, Cambridge University Press.
Not a book for the average layman or for students not conversant with modern linguistic theory. It contains a selection of the thoughts on pidgins and creoles by some of the greatest authorities in the world today. Invaluable for the specialist.
REINECKE, JOHN (1938) 'Trade jargons and creole dialects as marginal languages', *Social Forces*, vol. 17, pp. 107–18.
Reprinted in Hymes, *Language in Culture and Society*, New York, Harper & Row, 1964, pp. 134–46.
One of the earliest and still one of the most valuable brief analyses of the pidgin/creole phenomenon.
SCHUCHARDT, HUGO (1909) 'Die Lingua Franca', *Zeitschrift für romanische Philologie*, vol. 33, pp. 441–61.

Schuchardt was one of the first scholars to show interest in and an appreciation of pidgins and creoles. The article provides useful information for assessing the monogenetic theory.

THOMPSON, R. W. (1961) 'A note on some possible affinities between the creole dialects of the old world and those of the new', *Proceedings of the Conference on Creole Language Studies* (held at the University College of the West Indies, 28 March to 4 April 1959). Ed R. B. Le Page, London, Macmillan.

This brief article has inspired a great deal of research. It was among the first to see a Portuguese pidgin behind many non-Portuguese pidgins and creoles.

TURNER, LORENZO D. (1949) *Africanisms in the Gullah Dialect*, Chicago University Press.

Useful from the point of view of providing data on a rapidly changing creole and also because of its historical importance in connecting US black English with African influence.

WHINNOM, KEITH (1965) 'The origin of the European-based creoles and pidgins', *Orbis*, vol. 14, pp. 509–27.

A well documented argument in support of the monogenetic theory, particularly useful in view of his wide experience of Iberian-based pidgins and creoles.

Bibliography

The following lists are intended not as a comprehensive bibliography of works relating to pidgins and creoles, but as details of the references cited in the chapters of this book.

1 *Works published before 1900, and other source books*

ACHEBE, CHINUA (1960) *No Longer at Ease*, London, Heinemann. (African Writers Series, No. 3.)
— (1972) *Girls at War*, London, Heinemann. (African Writers Series, No. 100.)
ACOSTA, J. P. DE (1590) *Historia Natural y Moral de las Indas*, Sevilla, J. de Leon. B.M. ref. 146. a. 3. Reprinted from the English translated edition by Edward Grimstone (1604), and edited with notes and an introduction by C. R. Markham in *Hakluyt Society Works*, vols 60 and 61, London, 1880.
BARBOT, JOHN (1746) 'A Description of the Coasts of North and South Guinea', in *A Collection of Voyages and Travels*, vol. 5, ed. J. and A. Churchill, in six volumes, London, Henry Linton and John Osborn, 1744–6. (B.M. ref. 455, f. 1–6.)
BATES, HENRY W. (1863) *The Naturalist in the River Amazon*, London, John Murray. (B.M. ref. 10481, d. 14.) Reprinted unabridged, ed Edward Clodd, London, John Murray, 1892. (B.M. ref. 2374. f. 1.)
BERNCASTLE, JULIUS (1850) *A Voyage to China*, London, William Schoberl. (B.M. ref. 10055. c. 29.)
CHILD, F. J. ed. (1962) *The English and Scottish Popular Ballads*, New York, Cooper Square Publishers.
CRONISE, G. and WARD, H. F. (1903) *Cunnie Rabbit, Mister Spider and the Other Beef*, London, Sonnenschein.
CRUIKSHANK, G. (1819) an illustrated caricature from *Pigmy Revels or All Alive at Lilliput*, plate 2, ref. no. 9636, *Catalogue of Political and Personal Satires*, vol. vii, ed M. D. George, London, British Museum, 1942.
DAMPIER, WILLIAM (1697) *A New Voyage Round the World*, London, James Knapton. (B.M. ref. 1045. f. 1.) Reprinted with

an introduction by Sir Albert Grey, London, A. & C. Black, 1937.
DASENT, J. R. ed. (1890) *Acts of the Privy Council*, vol. 26, 1596–7, London, HMSO.
DEFOE, DANIEL (1719) *Farther Adventures of Robinson Crusoe*, Shakespeare Head edn, Oxford, Blackwell, 1927.
— (1722) *The History and Remarkable Life of the Truly Honourable Colonel Jacque*. Ed Samuel Holt Monk, London, Oxford University Press, 1965.
EDWARDS, BRYAN (1807) *The History, civil and commercial, of the British Colonies in the West Indies*, London, Stockdale. (This book is still readily available in university or good public libraries.)
HAMILTON, ALEXANDER (1727) *A New Account of the East Indies*, Edinburgh, J. Mosman. (B.M. ref. 793. e. 16.17.) Edited, with an introduction and notes, by Sir William Foster, London, Argonaut Press, 1930.
JONES, C. C. Jr (1888) *Negro Myths from the South Georgia Coast*, Detroit, Singing Tree Press.
LABARTHE, P. (1803) *Voyage à la Côte du Guinée*, Paris. (B.M. ref. 978. h. 13.)
LELAND, CHARLES (1876) *Pidgin English Sing-Song*, London, Trubner. (B.M. ref. 11688. aaa. 42.) (It was very popular in its day, and is still available in many university libraries.)
MILNE-HORNE, M. P. (1890) *Mamma's Black Nurse Stories*, Edinburgh, Blackwood. (B.M. ref. 12806. dd. 33.)
MOLIÈRE, J. B. P. DE (1670) *Le Bourgeois Gentilhomme*. In *Oeuvres Complètes*, vol. 2, Paris, Editions Gallimard, 1971.
NOBLE, C. F. (1747) *Voyage to the East Indies in 1747 and 1748*, London. (B.M. ref. 980. 1. 21.)
NUNN, HENRY PRESTON VAUGHAN (1966) *Lady Nugent's Journal of her Residence in Jamaica from 1801 to 1805*, ed P. Wright, Oxford, Blackwell.
PHILLIPS, THOMAS (1746) 'A Journal of a Voyage made in 1693, 1694' in *A Collection of Voyages and Travels*, vol. 6, ed J. and A. Churchill, in six volumes, London, Henry Linton and John Osborn, 1744–6. (B.M. ref. 455. f. 1–6.)
PLISSONEAU, JEAN (1926) *Catéchisme*, Metz, Louis Hellenbrand.
PURCHAS, SAMUEL (1625) *Purchas his Pilgrimes*, London, printed by William Stansby for Henrie Fetherstone. (B.M. ref. 679. h. 11–14.) Reprinted in twenty volumes by James MacLehose & Sons, Glasgow, 1905–7.
SAINT-QUENTIN, ALFRED et AUGUSTE DE (1872) *Introduction à*

l'histoire de Cayenne suivi d'un recueil de contes, fables at chansons en créole, Antibes.

SMITH, P. C. (1899) *Annancy Stories*, New York, R. H. Russell. (B.M. ref. 12806. dd. 33.)

THOMAS, J. J. (1869) *The Theory and Practice of Creole Grammar*, Port of Spain, Trinidad, The Chronicle Publishing Office. Reprinted with an introduction by Gertrud Buscher, London and Port of Spain, Beacon Books, 1969.

TROLLOPE, ANTHONY (1859) *The West Indies and the Spanish Main*, London, Chapman and Hall. (B.M. ref. 2374. d. 3.)

VEGA, CARCILASO DE LA (1609) *Royal Commentaries of the Incas and General History of Peru*, trans. H. V. Livermore, London, University of Texas Press, 1966.

WILSON, JOHN (1625) 'The Relation of Master John Wilson of Wanstead in Essex, one of the last ten that returned into England from Wiapoco in Guinea 1606', in *Purchas his Pilgrimes*, Book 4, ch. 14. London, printed by William Stansby for Henrie Fetherstone. (B.M. ref. 679. h. 11–14.) Reprinted in twenty volumes by James MacLehose & Sons, Glasgow, 1905–7.

2 *Dictionaries*

Dictionnaire de la Langue Franque ou Petit Mauresque (1830) (B.M. ref. 12907. a. 26.)

Oxford English Dictionary, London, Oxford University Press, 1933.

Oxford English Dictionary Supplement, London, Oxford University Press, 1972.

3 *Modern writing related to the study of pidgins and creoles*

ALEXANDRE, PIERRE (1962) 'Aperçu sommaire sur le Pidgin A 70 du Cameroun', *Symposium on Multilingualism*, pp. 251–65. Second meeting of the Inter-African Committee on Linguistics, Brazzaville, 16–21 July, 1962. Published by CCTA/CSA, publication no. 87, London, 1964.

BAILEY, B. L. (1966) *Jamaican Creole Syntax*, Cambridge University Press.

BERRY, JACK (1962) 'Pidgins and creoles in Africa', *Symposium on Multilingualism*, pp. 219–25. Second meeting of the Inter-African Committee on Linguistics, Brazzaville, 16–21 July, 1962. Published by CCTA/CSA, publication no. 87, London, 1964.

BLOOMFIELD, L. (1933) *Language*, London, Allen & Unwin.

BROCH, O. (1927) 'Russenorsk', *Archiv für Slawische Philologie*, vol. 41, pp. 209–62.

BROWN, R. and BELLUGI, U. (1964) 'Three Processes in the Child's Acquisition of Syntax', in *New Directions in the Study of Language*, ed E. Lenneberg, London, M.I.T. Press, pp. 131–61.

CARR, ELIZABETH B. (1972) *Da Kine Talk: From Pidgin to Standard English in Hawaii*, Hawaii University Press.

CARROLL, J. B. (1964) *Language and Thought*, Hemel Hempstead, Prentice-Hall.

CASSIDY, F. G. (1961) *Jamaica Talk: Three Hundred Years of the English Language in Jamaica*, London, Macmillan.

CHOMSKY, NOAM (1968) *Language and Mind*, New York, Harcourt Brace Jovanovitch.

CRAIG, D. (1966) 'Teaching English to Jamaican Creole Speakers', *Journal of Applied Linguistics*, vol. xvi, nos 1 and 2, pp. 49–60.

— (1971) 'Education and Creole English in the West Indies: Some Sociolinguistic Factors', in *Pidginization and Creolization of Languages*, ed Dell Hymes, Cambridge University Press, pp. 371–91.

DALBY, DAVID (1970a) *Black Through White: Patterns of Communication*, Bloomington, University of Indiana African Studies Program.

— (1970b) 'Jazz, Jitter and Jam', *The New York Times*, Tuesday, 10 November, p. 47.

DILLARD, JOHN L. (1972) *Black English*, New York, Random House.

EERSEL, CHRISTIAN (1971) 'Prestige in Choice of Language and Linguistic Form', in *Pidginization and Creolization of Languages*, ed Dell Hymes, Cambridge University Press, pp. 141–50.

EFRON, EDITH (1954) 'French and Creole Patois in Haiti', *Caribbean Quarterly*, vol. 3, no. 4, pp. 199–213.

FERGUSON, CHARLES (1959) 'Diglossia', *Word*, vol. 15, pp. 325–40.

— (1971) 'Absence of Copula and the Notion of Simplicity: a Study of Normal Speech, Baby Talk, Foreigner Talk and Pidgins', in *Pidginization and Creolization of Languages*, ed Dell Hymes, Cambridge University Press, pp. 141–50.

FORDE, C. DARYLL (1956) *Efik Traders of Old Calabar*, London, Oxford University Press.

GOODMAN, MORRIS F. (1964) *A Comparative Study of Creole French Dialects*, The Hague, Mouton.

— (1971) 'The Strange Case of Mbugu', in *Pidginization and*

104 Bibliography

Creolization of Languages, ed Dell Hymes, Cambridge University Press, pp. 243–54.

HALL, ROBERT A. Jr (1943) *Melanesian Pidgin English*, Baltimore, Linguistic Society of America.

— (1944) 'Chinese Pidgin English: grammar and texts', *Journal of the American Oriental Society*, vol. 64, pp. 95–113.

— (1966) *Pidgin and Creole Languages*, Ithaca, Cornell University Press.

HANCOCK, IAN F. (1972) *A List of Place Names in the Pacific North-West derived from the Chinook Jargon with a Word-list of the Language*, pub. Vancouver Public Library.

— and TODD, LORETO (1974) 'Pidgin's puzzling pedigree', *Journal of African Languages*, ed I. F. Hancock, vol. 12, no. 1.

HASSERT, KURT E. (1913) *Allgemeine Verkehrsgeographie*, Berlin and Leipzig, G. J. Göeschen'sceh Verlagshandlung.

HOGBIN, H. IAN (1939) *Experiments in Civilization*, London, Routledge & Kegan Paul.

HYMES, DELL ed. (1971) *Pidginization and Creolization of Languages*, Cambridge University Press.

JAKOBSON, ROMAN (1968) *Child Language, Aphasia and Phonological Universals*, New York, Humanities Press.

JESPERSEN, OTTO (1922) *Language: Its Nature, Development and Origin*, London, Allen & Unwin.

JONES, ELDRED (1971) 'Krio: an English-based Language of Sierra Leone', in *The English Language in West Africa*, ed John Spencer, London, Longman, pp. 66–94.

KLEINECKE, DAVID (1959) 'An etymology for "Pidgin" ', *International Journal of Applied Linguistics*, vol. 25, pp. 271–2.

LENNEBERG, ERIC (1964) 'A Biological Perspective of Language', in *New Directions in the Study of Language*, ed Eric Lenneberg, London, M.I.T. Press.

MATTHEWS, WILLIAM (1935) 'Sailors' pronunciation in the second half of the seventeenth century', *Anglia*, vol. 47, pp. 192–251.

MENCKEN, H. L. (1963) *The American Language*, ed R. I. McDavid, Jr and D. W. Maurer, London, Routledge & Kegan Paul.

MIHALIC, F. (1957) *Pidgin English (Neo-Melanesian) Dictionary and Grammar*, Techny, Illinois, The Mission Press, S.V.D.

MOSER, GERALD M. (1969) 'African literature in Portuguese: the first written, the last discovered', *African Forum*, vol. 2, no. 4, pp. 78–96.

MURPHY, JOHN J. (1966) *The Book of Pidgin English*, Brisbane, Smith & Paterson.

REINECKE, JOHN (1938) 'Trade Jargons and Creole Dialects as Marginal Languages', in *Language in Culture and Society*, ed Dell Hymes, New York, Harper & Row, 1964, pp. 534–46.

REISMAN, KARL (1970) 'Cultural and Linguistic Ambiguity in a West Indian Village', in *Afro-American Anthropology, Contemporary Perspectives*, ed N. E. Whitten and J. F. Szwed, New York, Free Press, pp. 129–44.

RENS, L. L. E. (1953) *The Historical and Social Background of Surinam Negro English*, Amsterdam, North-Holland Publishing Company.

ROSS, A. S. C. and MOVERLY, A. W. (1964) *The Pitcairnese Language*, London, André Deutsch.

RUDIN, HARRY (1938) *Germans in the Cameroons 1884–1914*, Westport, Negro Universities Press.

SAMARIN, W. (1967) *A Grammar of Sango*, The Hague, Mouton.

SELVON, SAMUEL (1965) *The Housing Lark*, London, MacGibbon & Kee.

SPENCER, JOHN ed. (1971) *The English Language in West Africa*, London, Longman.

STEWART, WILLIAM A. (1968) 'Continuity and change in American Negro Dialects', *Florida Foreign Language Reporter*, vol. 6, no. 1, pp. 3–14.

SYLVAIN, SUZANNE (1936) *Le Créole Haitien, morphologie et syntaxe*, Port-au-Prince, Haiti, Wetteren. (B.M. ref. 12911, dd. 19.)

TAYLOR, DOUGLAS (1971) 'Grammatical and Lexical Affinities of Creoles', in *Pidginization and Creolization of Languages*, ed Dell Hymes, Cambridge University Press, pp. 293–6.

TODD, LORETO (1973) Review of Carr's *Da Kine Talk: From Pidgin to Standard English in Hawaii* in *Journal of Linguistics*, vol. 10, no. 1.

— (1974) 'An analysis of the BE-verb in Cameroon Pidgin', *Archivum Linguisticum*, vol. 4, pp. 1–15.

TURNER, L. D. (1949) *Africanisms in the Gullah Dialect*, Chicago University Press.

VALKHOFF, MARIUS F. (1966) *Studies in Portuguese and Creole*, Johannesburg, Witwatersrand University Press.

— (1972) *New Light on Afrikaans and Malayo-Portuguese*, Louvain, Editions Peeters Imprimerie Orientaliste.

VINCENT, THEO (1972) 'Pidgin in Nigerian Literature', paper presented to the UNESCO Conference on Creole Languages and Educational Development, Trinidad, July, 1972.

VOORHOEVE, JAN (1971) 'The Art of Reading Creole Poetry', in *Pidginization and Creolization of Languages*, ed Dell Hymes, Cambridge University Press.

WEBSTER, G. (1960) 'Korean Bamboo English once more', *American Speech*, vol. 35, pp. 261–5.

WHINNOM, KEITH (1971) 'Linguistic Hybridization and the "Special Case" of Pidgins and Creoles', in *Pidginization and Creolization of Languages*, ed Dell Hymes, Cambridge University Press, pp. 91–115.

WOLFERS, E. (1971) 'A Report on Neo-Melanesian', in *Pidginization and Creolization of Languages*, ed Dell Hymes, Cambridge University Press, pp. 413–19.

WURM, S. A. (1971) 'Pidgins, Creoles and Lingue Franche', *Current Trends in Linguistics*, vol. 8, ed T. Sebeok, pp. 999–1021.

— and HARRIS, J. (1963) *Police Motu: An Introduction to the Trade Language of Papua*, Linguistic Circle of Canberra, Series 1, 1.